100 BUTTERCREAM
Flowers

Valeri Valeriano
& Christina Ong

**THE COMPLETE STEP-BY-STEP GUIDE TO
PIPING FLOWERS IN BUTTERCREAM ICING**

www.stitchcraftcreate.co.uk

D&C
David and Charles

CONTENTS

Introduction

This book is like our cake journey. If you have read our first book, *The Contemporary Buttercream Bible*, you will remember our first ever buttercream encounter – we piped a sunflower using a Ziploc bag as an improvised piping bag. The results were not great. But then we put clear tape around the end of the bag and cut a V shape for an instant nozzle, and a few moments after, Queen of Hearts Couture Cakes was founded! From that first 'beautiful' sunflower cupcake, we instantly became obsessed with piping. We learned how to pipe two more flowers... then five... then eight.. and now, 100!

Our love of colour has made us treasure beautiful flowers as inspirations for planning our cake designs. A few years ago, we started our 'Flowers To Do List' as a prompt to try to learn how to pipe as many flowers as we could, but we never really thought that the day would come when we would reach our target of 100 flowers and fulfil our ambition to put them in a book. The flowers here are all inspired by real flowers. Despite the fact that there are specific nozzles to use for so many different effects, there have still been some limitations in achieving anatomically correct flowers. This though does not affect the beauty of all the edible masterpieces in this book.

Three years ago we were scared to work on anything bigger than a cupcake because we thought a full-sized cake would be too complicated, but as we practised we gained confidence and became brave enough to decorate a small cake, and now

we're happy to tackle multi-tiered cakes. So we thought, in this book, we would also start small by decorating cupcakes, and by the end of it we hope that you too will find yourselves decorating towering cakes. We have also included five full-sized cake projects in this book, to show you how to apply your newly found piping skills on a bigger scale. Furthermore, we have showed how to pipe the flowers in clusters because this is a technique in itself. To pipe a single flower is easy, but to group them can be challenging – so we've got this covered for you.

There are loads of nozzles available and ways to pipe different effects, but in this book we have tried to simplify things for you so even if you are a beginner, you only have to practise and master our basic petal strokes, and you will be able to create all 100 flowers, and even more than that. When you have mastered the strokes, go ahead and explore other nozzles for variety, or try using bigger ones. You should also experiment with different brands of food colouring pastes and gels. Understanding colour mixing is very helpful when you want to achieve the right shades.

We hope that this book will inspire you to make not just one or two flowers, or even 100, but practise, practise and a little bit more practise is all you need!

Buttercream Basics

BASIC BUTTERCREAM RECIPE

With this recipe, the one thing you should remember is never over-beat your buttercream. If you do it will become grainy and the edges of your petals are likely to 'break' when you pipe your flowers.

A hand-held mixer is not usually as powerful as a stand mixer, so if you are using a hand-held mixer, make sure you fold your mixture manually first until the ingredients are incorporated. This helps to avoid over-beating as well.

What is so good about our recipe is that a little less or more of a certain ingredient is fine. So if your buttercream is too stiff, add water or milk. If it is too thin, just add icing (confectioners') sugar. Adjust it as you need to – all in moderation, of course. You may use your buttercream straight away to cover and decorate your cakes but we suggest you chill it in the fridge for about an hour for the best results.

ABOUT VEGETABLE FAT, AKA SHORTENING
This is a white solid fat made from vegetable oils, and is usually flavourless or at least bland. It plays a very important role in our recipe as it helps make our buttercream stable. It also allows the surface of the decorated cake to 'crust' so that it is not too sticky. And since it makes it stable, you do not need to add too much icing sugar to make a stiff consistency, thus your frosting has just the right sweetness.

Different brands of vegetable fat (shortening) have different consistencies. If the consistency of your shortening is somewhat medium-soft to slightly hard, like Trex, use 113g (4oz) in the recipe below. If it is soft and very spreadable, like Crisco, you will have to double the amount to 227g (8oz).

You will need...

- 227g (8oz) butter, room temperature
- 113g (4oz) medium soft vegetable fat (shortening) (Trex), at room temperature, OR 227g (8oz) of soft spreadable vegetable fat (Crisco)
- 2–3 tsp vanilla essence, or your choice of flavouring
- 1 tbsp water or milk (omit if you live in a hot country or whenever the temperature is hot)
- 600g (1lb 5oz) icing (confectioners') sugar, sifted, if you are using medium soft vegetable fat OR 750g (1lb 10oz) icing sugar, sifted, if you are using soft spreadable vegetable fat
- Mixer (hand-held or stand mixer)
- Mixing bowls
- Spatula
- Sieve (sifter/strainer)
- Measuring spoons

1. Beat the butter at medium speed until soft and pale (about one to two minutes). Some brands of butter are more yellow in colour, so to make it paler you can increase the beating time to about two to five minutes.

2. Add the vegetable fat (shortening) and beat for another 20 to 30 seconds or less. Make sure that it is well incorporated and that there are no lumps.

Important: As soon as you add anything to the butter, you must limit your beating time to 20–30 seconds or even less.

3. Add vanilla essence, or your flavour of choice and water, or milk, then beat at medium speed for about 10 to 20 seconds until well incorporated.

4. Slowly add the sifted icing (confectioners') sugar and beat at medium speed for another 20 to 30 seconds or until everything is combined.

You may want to fold the ingredients together manually before beating to avoid puffing clouds of sugar round your kitchen. Make sure you scrape the sides and bottom of your bowl, as well as the blade of your mixer, so you don't miss any lumps of icing sugar.

5. Lastly, after scraping the bowl, beat again for about 20 to 30 seconds and do not over-mix. This yields a perfect piping consistency for buttercream.

TIP
You may add milk, but if you do you can only keep your buttercream for two to four days, as milk has a shorter shelf-life. If you use water, you will be able to keep it for longer – about five to ten days.

ADDING FLAVOURS
Flavoured buttercream will add character to your cake, and there are plenty of options to choose from: cocoa powder, fruit jam (jelly), peanut butter, squashed berries or even green tea to name a few. Just be mindful of consistency – make a batch of buttercream as described here then add your flavouring, you can add a little water or icing sugar at the end to adjust the stiffness. Beware of squashed berries or fruit, which may have a high water content and can make your buttercream very runny. If this is the case, you can omit the water or vanilla essence to reduce the liquid content.

COVERAGE
If you make the basic buttercream recipe with the amounts given, one batch will yield approximately 1–1.1kg (2lb 7½oz) of buttercream. This will be enough to cover the top, the sides and fill a 20cm (8in) round or square cake, or decorate about 20–30 cupcakes, depending on the design. This can be your guide to determine how much frosting you need to prepare. If you have any buttercream left over, just label it with the date you made it and store it in the fridge.

TIP
Keep your buttercream inside the refrigerator (chiller) and store it in an air-tight container or food storage bags. You can freeze it for up to a month, letting it defrost thoroughly at room temperature before use. Do not beat it again in a mixer, just mix it manually. But of course, nothing is better than fresh buttercream!

EQUIPMENT

To create great cakes you need the right equipment, and we've gathered together the tools of our trade here. You won't need everything pictured below, but use our advice in the flower instructions and cake projects in this book to select the items that you need to get the best results.

1 Cake leveller
2 Serrated/straight knives
3 Sieve (sifter/strainer)
4 Scissors
5 Ruler
6 Spatulas
7 Cake turntable
8 Greaseproof (wax) paper and cling film
9 Measuring cups/spoons
10 Couplers

11 Disposable piping (pastry) bags
12 Palette knife
13 Flower nail
14 Cake scraper
15 Mixing bowls
16 Tweezers
17 Nozzles
18 Food colouring pastes and gels
19 Weighing scales
20 Hand-held mixer

21 Stand mixer
22 Cupcake tin
23 Airbrush machine
24 Cupcake liners
25 Tall glass
26 Gold dragees
27 Cocktail sticks
28 Cake boards and cards
29 Interfacing cloth
30 Headed pins

NOZZLES

Nozzles, or piping tips, can produce all the effects that you need to create amazingly realistic flowers. They come in different sizes and brands, and each brand has its corresponding numbers or letters inscribed on it to indicate its output. We've indicated which nozzles you need in each of the flower instructions that follow, but here's a general guide to show you which nozzle does what.

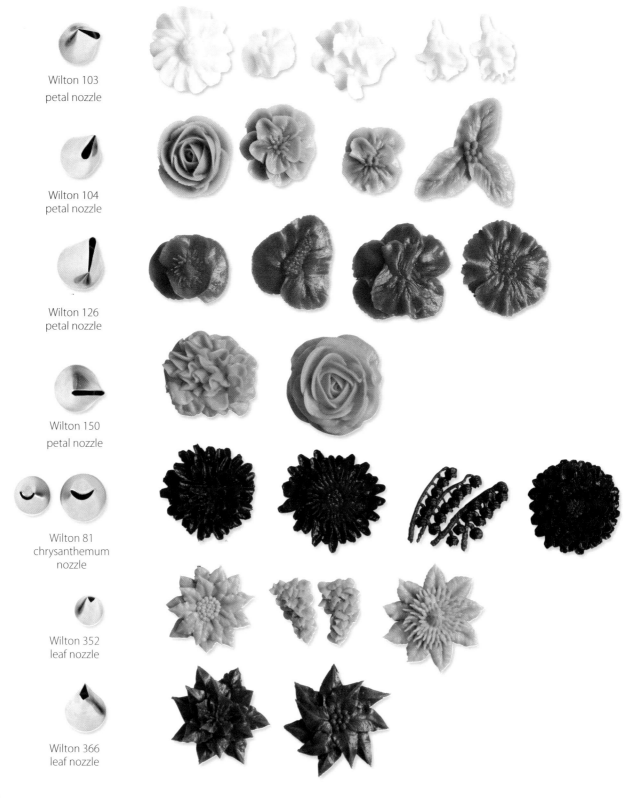

Wilton 103
petal nozzle

Wilton 104
petal nozzle

Wilton 126
petal nozzle

Wilton 150
petal nozzle

Wilton 81
chrysanthemum
nozzle

Wilton 352
leaf nozzle

Wilton 366
leaf nozzle

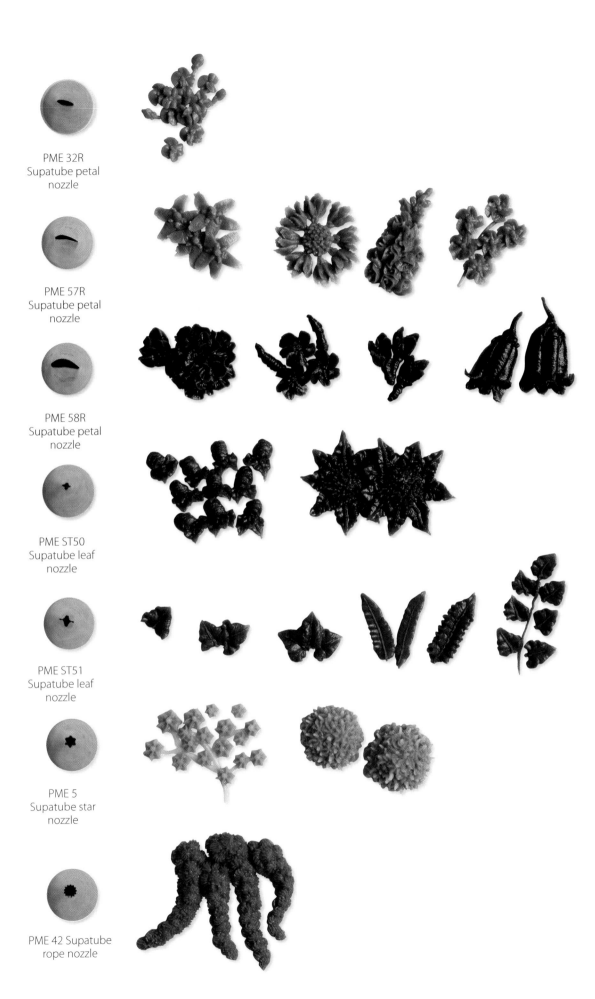

PME 32R
Supatube petal
nozzle

PME 57R
Supatube petal
nozzle

PME 58R
Supatube petal
nozzle

PME ST50
Supatube leaf
nozzle

PME ST51
Supatube leaf
nozzle

PME 5
Supatube star
nozzle

PME 42 Supatube
rope nozzle

COLOURING

Mixing colours plays a vitally important role in cake decorating. Colours bring your cake to life, can set a mood, attract attention or make a statement. Hence, it is important to choose and prepare your tinted buttercream properly. Try to learn a little about colour theory, there's plenty of information and examples of it on the Internet. Take inspiration from real flowers, the dresses in your wardrobe, wallpapers, gift wrapping and anything beautiful to help you choose colours that will make your cake design spectacular.

We have highlighted below the things you should remember when mixing colours·

- Make sure that your buttercream is at room temperature when tinting, so that the colours blend together.

- Add paste colours a little at a time using a clean cocktail stick (toothpick), and never re-use it. Or tint a small amount of buttercream to create a strong colour, then use that to add to your bigger batch of buttercream so that you can control the strength of colour gradually.

- When tinting buttercream, mix it manually. *Do not* put it into the mixer to blend it even if it is a huge amount because there is a risk that you will over-beat it.

- Bear in mind that it is normal for buttercream to deepen in colour after a short while, especially with darker colours. Prepare it at least two or three hours ahead of time to allow for any colour change.

- Prepare more than enough tinted buttercream for big projects. You don't want a part of your cake to be a different colour, do you?

- If you are aiming for a dark colour, such as black, navy blue or a dark red, you will need to add more colouring gel or paste, so omit the the water or milk to prevent the buttercream becoming too runny, or add them after you have mixed your desired colour.

- If your buttercream is a little yellowish, you can make it whiter by adding a hint of violet or a whitener, such as Sugarflair Super White. If you are aiming for a light shade, whiten the buttercream first then add the desired colour.

- If the colours that you have made are very bright, you can tone them down by adding a hint of black, brown or violet.

- Food colouring comes as powder, liquid, gel or paste. *Do not* use powder food colour to tint your buttercream directly as it will not dissolve properly. When mixed, it will look as if it is well blended but after a while, the tiny granules will start to dissolve and will show speckles of colours. If this is your only option, we suggest that you dissolve the powder in a very small drop of water, bearing in mind that the more liquid you put in buttercream, the softer it becomes.

- If you are using a liquid food colouring like those in squeeze bottles, it is sometimes hard to control the amount that comes out, especially if you need even less than a drop. You can tint a small amount of buttercream then use that to add colour to your bigger batch, rather than putting colours directly to your buttercream.

- Food colouring pastes and gels come in many different brands and each has a different concentration and yields a different shade. Whatever brand you have locally, you should always try it first in a small batch so as to prevent wasting the buttercream.

SOME COLOUR MIXING EXAMPLES

Here's how to make some of the colours that you might want. Bear in mind that different manufacturers will have different names for their own colours, so only generic names have been given here.

Gold = lemon yellow (any bright yellow) + orange

Red = dark pink + orange + red (+ brown/black for deep red)

Avocado = lemon yellow + leaf green + hint of black

Turquoise = electric blue + leaf green

Coral = pink + yellow

Black (centre) = brown + black (or black extra)

Plum = violet + hint of red

Rust = orange + hint of red + hint of brown

Lavender = pink + violet

Navy blue = dark blue + black

Mauve = violet + yellow

Deep purple = bright red or pink + hint of violet

COVERING CAKES

Before you can add an amazing floral decoration, you need to know how to cover your cake, making sure that the buttercream sticks to it and provides a clean base. You need to first crumb coat, then create a smooth surface. Further techniques for creating textured or perfectly smooth surfaces can be found within the cake projects at the end of the book.

CRUMB COATING
This technique means applying a thin layer of buttercream around your cake to secure the loose crumbs. This is a very important step that you should not miss, as this makes your outer layer of buttercream stick to the cake, giving the heavy piped and textured designs something to adhere to.

A

B

1. You can use a palette knife to apply the buttercream to the cake, but some cake sponges can be very crumbly. When you use a palette knife, the tendency is to keep pushing and pressing the frosting and this might damage your cake. Instead, we use a piping bag to apply the frosting.

2. Use a round nozzle or just snip the end off a piping bag. Using the same frosting that will go on the rest of the cake, fill the piping bag (A) and pipe around the cake with a good pressure so it sticks to the cake (B).

3. Use your palette knife to spread the buttercream, using even pressure (C).

4. Next you can use a cake scraper to level out the thickness of the frosting and to remove any excess (D).

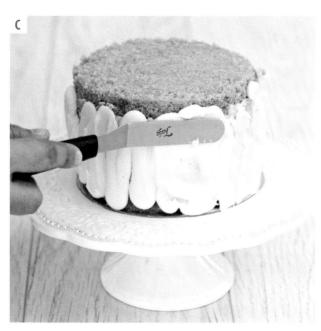
C

D

SMOOTHING

After the cake has been chilled for a short while you can apply another layer of buttercream and create a smooth surface. The thickness of this layer will be a matter of taste. To be able to produce a perfectly smooth a cake takes patience and practise. Trust us, you will not be able to 'perfectly perfect' it on your first go, but after a while you will get so practised at it that it will become easy.

PALETTE KNIFE

This is the common way of smoothing a cake – no fancy tool, just a palette knife. You simply have to spread the buttercream frosting around the cake using the knife. The finish though is not perfectly smooth as the knife will leave a few lines and ridges.

You can use any palette knife, straight or cranked, and the best choice of size will depend on the size of your cake. We find it is best to use a short crank-handled knife for most occasions. The direction in which you spread doesn't matter, but it is important to remove any excess buttercream and to make an even layer (A).

CAKE SCRAPER

Make sure that the edge of your scraper is perfectly smooth. Remember that any dent on your scraper will be visible on your cake because buttercream is soft and delicate. Using a plain edge scraper is a fairly quick way of smoothing your cake. With the cake on a turntable, hold the scraper upright and perpendicular to the work surface, and run it around your cake until smooth (B).

If your cake is tall you may need to use a longer implement, such as a ruler, a big cake lifter or (the most effective tool we've found) an L ruler or 90-degree triangle ruler.

A

B

FILLING A PIPING BAG

SINGLE COLOUR

For a single colour, use a tall glass or vase to support your piping bag then scoop the buttercream into it.

TIP

Do not over-fill your piping bag – you need to be able to get a good grip so that you can control the squeeze as you pipe, and also you don't want your hands to get tired.

TWO-TONE EFFECT

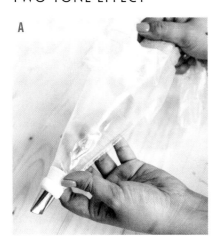

A

B

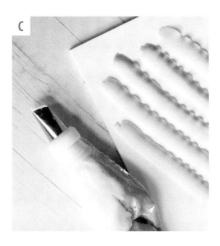

C

1. Prepare your tinted buttercream in two separate piping bags and cut a medium hole at the tip of each. The 'stripe' colour should be piped into a third bag, with the nozzle attached, where the narrow end of the nozzle is (A).

2. Pipe the dominant colour on top of the stripe colour to fill the bag (B).

3. Squeeze the piping bag until you get the right effect (C). To adjust the thickness of the stripe colour, just turn the nozzle clockwise or counter-clockwise.

BLENDED TWO-TONE EFFECT

1. Repeat the same process as for the two-tone effect but randomly pinch the part of the bag where the stripe colour mixes with the dominant colour to create a blended effect.

2. Squeeze the piping bag until you're happy with the effect.

THREE-TONE EFFECT

1. Fill three separate piping bags with your chosen shades of buttercream (A), and prepare a large piece of cling film (plastic wrap).

2. Cut a medium-sized hole at the tip of each of the piping bags and squeeze them onto the sheet of cling film in whatever order you like (B).

3. Roll the cling film up and make it like a sausage. Twist both ends and tie one end tightly (C).

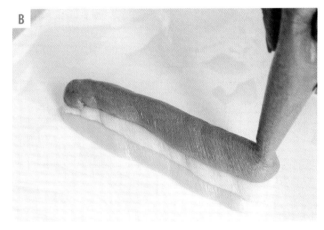

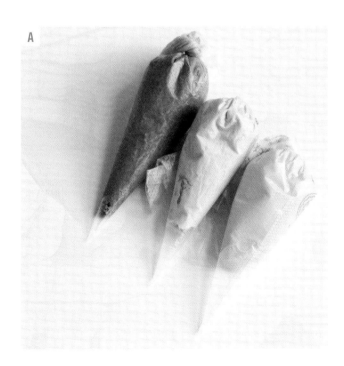

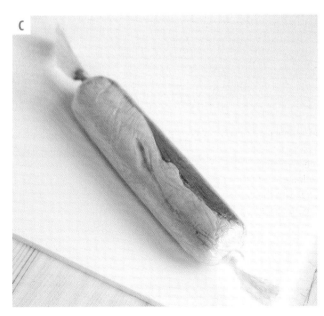

4. Prepare your piping bag with a coupler. Thread the twisted part of the cling film to the coupler, pull it through the opening and cut the end off, then attach the ring with the nozzle to the base of the coupler.

5. Squeeze the piping bag until you get the right effect. You may also try more than three colours using the same technique.

TIP
If you need a lot of buttercream, it's a good idea to prepare two full piping bags in advance.

MARBLED EFFECT

1. Prepare your chosen colours and place them in the same bowl (A).

2. Blend the colours lightly (B). Scoop the buttercream into your piping bag (C).

3. Squeeze the piping bag until you get the right effect (D).

TIP
Do not over-blend the buttercream as it will turn into one colour. You could use more than two colours. Untinted buttercream is usually a good third choice as it balances the other colours.

A

B

C

D
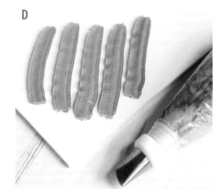

PIPING ADVICE

NOZZLE POSITION

The angle of the nozzle plays a very important role in flower piping. It is absolutely essential in ensuring that your petals are the right shape. Throughout the book you will repeatedly see 'position the nozzle at a 20 to 30 degree angle' as this is what we consider the basic position. The general rule is when piping petals you usually start at the outer layer and as you advance towards the centre of the flower, the angle of your nozzle increases in 5 to 10 degree increments. The nozzle should *always be touching the previous layer of petals.*

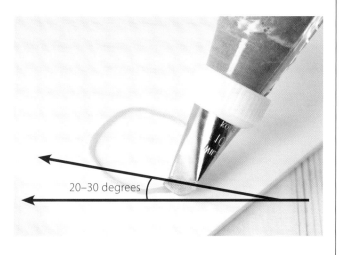

20–30 degrees

PRESSURE CONTROL

Control of the pressure you exert on the piping bag is another essential in piping. The amount of pressure you apply in squeezing your piping bag as well as the consistency of the pressure determines the size and uniformity of your petals or decoration. In flower piping, if you squeeze lightly, this can result in the edges of the petals breaking. If you squeeze too hard there is the tendency for the petals to curl or create a rather wavy effect, and a rather thick-looking petal will be the result. Practise until you have a good feel for the correct amount of pressure.

USING A FLOWER NAIL

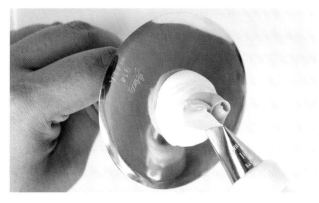

1. Holding your nozzle flat, squeeze the piping bag with firm, continuous pressure as you turn the flower nail to build up a mound of buttercream for a base. Then, pipe the flower on top.

2. Use scissors to cut through the base but do not fully close the scissors. Just make sure that the flower sits securely on the scissor blades then twist the nail and slide the flower away gently.

3. Use a palette knife or the back of a spoon to slide the flower off the nail.

1. Cut a small piece of greaseproof (wax) paper about 7–7.5cm (2–3in) square and stick it onto a flower nail with a small blob of buttercream.

2. Pipe your flower on the flower nail (see Using a Flower Nail) then use scissors to lift it up from underneath the greaseproof paper.

TIP

Do not freeze your piped flowers for long – definitely not overnight – as because of condensation, the flowers will sweat and this will sometimes will cause bleeding of the colours. Put them in the freezer for just 10 to 20 minutes or until the buttercream is firm to the touch.

3. Gently slide the rose onto a small board or tray, hold one corner of the greaseproof paper down with your finger then pull the scissors away. Freeze for 10 to 20 minutes, or keep checking until the flower is hard enough to touch.

BASIC PETAL STROKES

Some good news! All the flowers in this book can be created with just ten basic piping strokes. Master them by following the step-by-step instructions below, and refer back here as often as you need.

SIMPLE PETAL

1. Position the nozzle at a 20 to 30 degree angle with the wide end of the nozzle touching the surface and the narrow end pointing outwards. The narrow end of the nozzle should be in a 12 o'clock position.

2. Give the piping bag a good squeeze *without* moving or turning your hands or your piping bag. The wide end of nozzle should remain in the same position.

3. Release the pressure when the buttercream creates a simple petal shape.

4. Gently pull the piping bag down or towards you so that the petal has a clean edge.

FAN-SHAPED PETAL

1. Position the nozzle at a 20 to 30 degree angle with the wide end of nozzle touching the surface and the narrow end pointing outwards. The narrow end of the nozzle should start in a 10 o'clock position (2 o'clock for left-handers).

2. Squeeze the piping bag with constant, even pressure while slowly turning the nozzle to the right (or left for left-handers), to create the beginning of a small arch.

3. You will create a fan-shape, as the narrow end of nozzle points to around the 2 o'clock position, at this point release the pressure.

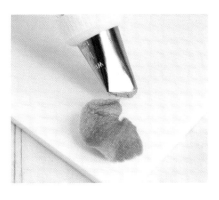

4. Gently pull the piping bag down or towards you so that the petal has a clean edge.

PULLED PETAL

1. For flowers that have pulled petals it is always helpful to pipe a guide circle. You can start anywhere and position the nozzle flat on the surface with the wide end touching your guide circle, or towards the centre of the flower.

2. Squeeze the piping bag with constant, even pressure while pulling away.

3. When you reach the length you want, release the pressure then abruptly pull away.

4. It is common for this type of petal to have a jagged tip when you have piped it. Just wait for the buttercream to crust a little bit and use a cocktail stick to smooth the edges.

RUFFLE PETAL

1. Position the nozzle at a 20 to 30 degree angle with the wide end of the nozzle touching the surface and narrow end pointing outwards.

2. Squeeze the piping bag with constant, even pressure as you move your hand in a slight up and down motion while gradually moving clockwise (counter-clockwise for left-handers).

3. Continue to pipe until you reach the desired length of petal. You may stop at any point and just join the petals again should you need to make it longer.

4. Gently pull the piping bag down or towards you so the petal has a clean edge.

LONG CURVED PETAL

1. Position the nozzle at a 20 to 30 degree angle with the wide end of the nozzle touching the surface and the narrow end pointing outwards.

2. Squeeze the piping bag with constant, even pressure as you move your hand in a long curved motion, clockwise (counter clockwise for left-handers).

3. Continue to pipe until you reach the desired length of petal.

4. Gently pull the piping bag down or towards you so the petal has clean edge.

TWO-STROKE PETAL

1. Start piping one side of the petal by positioning your nozzle facing left, and positioned flat on the surface.

2. Squeeze the piping bag with constant, even pressure in a jiggling up and down motion until you reach the tip of your petal.

3. To create a pointed petal, pull the piping bag away when you reach the tip. To create a rounded tip go to step 5.

4. Turn the nozzle to the right while keeping the wide end to the centre of the petal making sure that there is no gap. Then continue with a jiggling up and down motion going back down to the base to create the other half of the petal.

5. To create a rounded tip, turn the piping bag straight after piping the first side of the petal, then continue piping the other side of the petal.

6. You can use this technique to create a smooth petal by simply omitting the jiggling motion as you pipe.

HEART-SHAPED PETAL

1. Position the nozzle flat with the wide end touching the surface and the narrow end pointing outwards. The narrow end of the nozzle should start in a 10 o'clock position (2 o'clock for left-handers).

2. Squeeze the piping bag with light even and constant pressure then gradually pull up to the length you require. Carefully turn halfway to the right, release the pressure, and pull the nozzle down.

3. Pipe the other half of the petal by positioning your nozzle where the first stroke ended. Then squeeze the piping bag making a slight curve, the same height as the first.

4. Pull the nozzle down to the base.

UPRIGHT PETAL

1. Hold the piping bag at a 90 degree angle with the opening of the nozzle facing downwards towards the surface.

2. Give the piping bag a good squeeze until you get an upright looking petal. You can drag the nozzle downwards to create a longer petal. You can also slightly wiggle the nozzle to create a wavy petal.

3. Finish off the petal by pulling the nozzle down.

LEAF TECHNIQUE PETAL

1. Hold the piping bag at a 20 to 30 degree angle with one of the pointed ends of the nozzle touching the surface.

2. Squeeze the piping bag with constant even pressure until it creates a wide base.

3. Gradually pull the piping bag while continuously squeezing but gradually releasing pressure as you reach the desired length of your petal.

4. Once you reach the desired length, stop squeezing the bag and pull the nozzle abruptly.

UP DOWN PETAL

1. Hold the nozzle completely flat against the surface.

2. Squeeze evenly and move the piping bag to the desired petal length.

3. Make a tight turn to create a rounded tip, but do not make an arch.

4. With the same pressure, pull the piping bag back to the base of the petal.

FLOWERS

When we started our flower 'to do' list, we never imagined that we would design and pipe quite so many different blooms. When we reached 100 we felt we just had to share them with others, so here they are: organized by colour and broken down into simple steps to make them achievable whatever your level of expertize. Remember to refer back to the Basic Petal Strokes whenever you need to.

Make sure that you always pipe the leaves or sepals first before you pipe the main petals on top, help with leaves and other greenery can be found at the end of the flowers section.

Calla Lily

These large flowers with thick, curved petals are usually cut and brought indoors for use in bold and beautiful arrangements. Most commonly white, the calla lily is particularly popular for weddings.

To create this flower...

- Colours: for the petals, white (Sugarflair Super White); for the centre, yellow (Sugarflair Yellow plus Autumn Leaf); for the calyx and stem, green (Sugarflair Gooseberry)
- Wilton Petal Nozzle 104/126
- Piping bags

1. Start with a simple pulled petal (see Basic Petal Strokes) about 2.5cm (1in) long, or longer depending on your design, with the nozzle narrow end up.

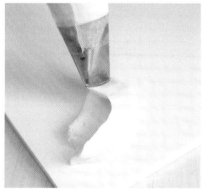

2. Position the nozzle on the right side of the pulled petal and pipe an upright petal from the tip to the base. Curve your petal towards the bottom then fold.

3. Pipe another upright petal on the left-hand side making sure that it creates a pointed tip…

4. … and that the bottom overlaps the first petal.

5. Cut a medium hole at the tip of a piping bag and pipe the flower centre in yellow, using steady pressure, gradually releasing the pressure towards the tip.

6. Use a piping bag with a small hole in the tip to pipe the green calyx and stems.

Gardenia

Each heavily fragranced gardenia bloom consists of frilly, somewhat waxy, white petals that radiate from the flower's centre.

To create this flower...

- Colours: for the petals, white (Sugarflair Super White); for the centre, yellow (Sugarflair Melon plus Autumn Leaf); for the stamens, brown (Sugarflair Brown plus a hint of Gooseberry)
- Wilton Petal Nozzle 104
- Flower nail (optional)
- Piping bags

1. Pipe a mound of buttercream, then hold the nozzle with its opening vertical. Squeeze the piping bag and turn the mound counter-clockwise to create a small upright petal (see Basic Petal Strokes).

2. Repeat, making sure that the petals overlap.

3. Build up the flower by piping arch-shaped upright petals, increasing the size as you work outwards. Add character by piping longer and slightly frilly petals.

4. If it is becoming difficult to pipe in one direction, you can swap and work clockwise.

5. Cut a small hole at the tip of the piping bag and pipe short, slightly wavy stamens using brown buttercream.

6. Using a piping bag with a small hole at the tip, pipe the centre in yellow using firm pressure on the piping bag.

Lily of the Valley

Clusters of small, white, bell-shaped flowers hang prettily from one side of a bright green stalk. Wonderfully fragrant, lily of the valley will brighten any area with its beauty and perfume.

To create this flower...

- Colours: for the petals, white (Sugarflair Super White); for the stems and leaves, light and dark green (Sugarflair Gooseberry)
- Wilton Nozzle 81 and Wilton Leaf Nozzle 352
- Piping bags

1. Pipe varying sizes of leaves in green buttercream with the leaf nozzle, using the leaf technique (see Basic Petal Strokes).

2. Using a piping bag with the tip snipped off and a slightly lighter green, pipe long stems with short curvy secondary stems growing outward from the main stem.

3. To create the white blossoms, hold the Wilton Nozzle 81 with the curved side touching a short stem. Squeeze with light, constant pressure and gently pull up until you create a small half-bell shape.

4. Repeat the same process and pipe blossoms on each of the short stems.

TIP
This is a very good filler flower. Make sure you pipe Lily of the Valley directly onto a cake if you intend to decorate it with other flowers too. Use different sizes of the Chrysanthemum nozzles to give variation to the flowers' shapes and sizes.

Magnolia

The blossoms of the magnolia are large and scented, and have between six and 12 petals. Magnolia flower arrangements are very sumptuous and elegant making them a favourite for special occasions.

To create this flower...

- Colours: for the petals, White (Sugarflair Super White); for the centre, green (Sugarflair Gooseberry); for the stamen, brown (Sugarflair Brown plus a hint of Gooseberry)
- Wilton Petal Nozzle 104
- Piping bags

1. Pipe a circle as a guide for size. Position your nozzle at a 20 to 30 degree angle, and steadily squeeze the piping bag to create a long curved petal (see Basic Petal Strokes).

2. Repeat until you have piped about five or six petals for the first layer.

3. For the next layer, pipe about four to six petals at a steeper angle, as close as possible to the first layer of petals.

4. Snip a small hole at the tip of a piping bag and pipe short spikes at the centre using green buttercream.

5. Pipe the stamen around the green centre in the same way, this time using brown buttercream.

Jasmine

The flowers of this heavily fragranced climber are tubular, while the glossy leaves have an oval shape. When the sun goes down the scent of the jasmine plant is at its most intoxicating.

To create this flower...

- Colours: for the buds and petals, white (Sugarflair Super White); for the stem and calyx, green (Sugarflair Gooseberry); for the centre, yellow (Sugarflair Melon)
- PME Petal Nozzle 58R
- Piping bags

1. Cut the tip of a piping bag to create a medium size hole. With firm pressure, pipe a few short thick lines randomly around where your flowers will be, to represent buds.

2. Using your green buttercream in a piping bag with a small hole at the tip, pipe a stem and calyx for each bud.

3. Pipe your first flower with the petal nozzle, by piping five simple petals (see Basic Petal Strokes) that join at one common central point.

4. Repeat, piping a few more flowers to create a lovely bunch.

5. Pipe the flower centres using yellow buttercream in a piping bag with a small hole at the tip.

Gypsophilia

Commonly known as 'baby's breath', gypsophilia can fill your garden with tiny clouds of white flowers. Each small flower has a delicate cup-like calyx of white-edged green sepals containing five petals.

To create this flower...

- Colours: for the petals, white (Sugarflair Super White); for the stem, green (Sugarflair Gooseberry)
- PME Petal Nozzles 5 and 7
- Piping bags

1. Pipe the stems using green buttercream in a piping bag with a small hole at the tip.

2. Hold the piping bag at a 90 degree angle with the nozzle (either 5 or 7) touching the surface. Squeeze the piping bag until it builds up and creates a flower, then pull away.

3. Repeat the same process to pipe small flowers randomly.

4. Swap to the other nozzle and repeat the same process to pipe more flowers, again in a random pattern.

5. Pipe the centre of each of the flowers using yellow buttercream in a piping bag with small hole snipped at the tip.

Frangipani

Also known as plumeria, frangipani have a wonderful tropical quality. Each flower has about five petals, which have a waxy finish, and a touch of yellow in the centre.

To create this flower...

- Colours: for the petals, white (Sugarflair Super White) and yellow (Sugarflair Melon plus Autumn Leaf); for the centre, darker yellow (Sugarflair Melon plus Autumn Leaf)
- Wilton Petal Nozzle 104
- Piping bags

1. Holding the piping bag at a 20 to 30 degree angle with the yellow buttercream at the bottom, pipe a short up-down petal (see Basic Petal Strokes).

2. Repeat and pipe four more petals all starting at the same central point.

3. To add character, and fill any slight gap in the centre, pipe a little darker yellow buttercream using a piping bag with a small hole in the tip.

4. To pipe the next flower in the cluster, pipe a blob of buttercream and repeat steps 1 to 3 on top of it.

TIP

For a different Frangipani colour, prepare a two-tone bag (see Two-tone Effect) with yellow at the wide end of the nozzle and light pink at the narrow end.) You may also use bigger nozzles, such as Wilton Petal 124, 125 or 126.

Daisy

The daisy is known as a composite flower, meaning it is made up of an arrangement of clusters of tiny flowers that give it the appearance of a single bloom.

To create this flower...

- Colours: for the petals, white (Sugarflair Super White); for the centre, yellow (Sugarflair Melon plus Autumn Leaf)
- Wilton Petal Nozzle 104
- Piping bags

1. Pipe a circle as a guide, then hold the nozzle flat to the surface with the wide end touching the guide. Take your white buttercream for the petals.

2. Give the piping bag a good squeeze and pipe an up-down petal (see Basic Petal Strokes).

3. Repeat the same process and pipe more petals, making sure that each one starts and ends on the guide circle.

4. Using your yellow buttercream in a piping bag with a medium hole cut at the tip, squeeze with even pressure and pipe in a spiral motion to create a slight dome.

5. To pipe another flower, pipe a blob of buttercream to help position the next flower, and repeat steps 1 to 4 on top.

Dogwood

Flowering dogwood is a small multi-branched tree with oval leaves that bears very beautiful snowy flowers. In truth the flowers are not large but appear big because of their four petal-like bracts, which are heart shaped.

To create this flower...

- Colours: for the petals, white (Sugarflair Super White); for the centre, light and dark green (Sugarflair Gooseberry) and yellow (Sugarflair Melon); for the stamen, brown (Sugarflair Brown and a hint of Gooseberry)
- Wilton Petal Nozzle 104
- Piping bags

1. Hold your piping bag at a 20 to 30 degree angle and pipe a heart-shaped petal (see Basic Petal Strokes).

2. Repeat the same process and pipe three more heart-shaped petals that meet at a central point.

3. Using your brown buttercream in a piping bag with small hole at the tip, pipe a V-shape on the edge of each petal to create a notch.

4. Pipe a small mound of dark green buttercream in the centre and pipe light green dots on top of it, using a piping bag with a small hole at the tip.

5. Add yellow dots in the centre, again with a piping bag with a small hole snipped at the tip.

6. To pipe another flower, pipe a blob of buttercream to position the next flower, and repeat steps 1 to 5 on top.

Narcissus

Bringing swathes of colour to woods and gardens, these cheerful spring flowers are characterized by a cup-like corona, surrounded by petals and sepals. Ever popular daffodils form part of the narcissus family.

To create this flower...

- Colours: for the petals, white (Sugarflair Super White); for the corona, yellow (Sugarflair Melon plus Autumn Leaf); for the centre, dark yellow (Sugarflair Melon plus Autumn Leaf)
- Wilton Petal Nozzle 104
- Piping bags

1. For a sideways facing narcissus, pipe two pulled petals in white to make a V-shape using a 104 nozzle.

2. Using yellow buttercream and the nozzle, pipe two folded petals by holding the piping bag flat to the surface, nozzle facing left, squeeze the piping bag as you pull away and fold back to the centre. Pipe dark yellow spikes using a piping bag with a small hole at the tip.

3. Pipe three more pulled petals that start from the base of the cup and swoop away, slightly curving each one back at the tip.

4. For a narcissus that faces upwards, pipe a guide circle and then six pulled petals that start in the centre.

5. Using yellow buttercream with the nozzle, pipe a rigid ruffle petal in the centre to form the cup.

6. Pipe the centre spikes using dark yellow buttercream in a piping bag with a small hole at the tip.

Cherry Blossom

Irresistibly pretty, cherry blossom has become an iconic symbol of springtime. Most have delicate single blossoms with five petals, but some are frilly affairs with up to 20 or more.

To create this flower...

- Colours: for the petals, pink (Sugarflair Baby Pink (Pastel)); for the twigs, brown (Sugarflair Dark Brown); for the centre, dark pink (Sugarflair Red); for the dots, yellow (Sugarflair Melon plus Autumn Leaf)
- Wilton Petal Nozzle 103
- Piping bags

1. Using brown buttercream, pipe the twigs using a piping bag with a medium-size hole cut at the tip.

2. Using the nozzle, pipe five simple petals (see Basic Petal Strokes) from a common central point.

3. Using your dark pink buttercream and piping bag with a small hole cut at the tip, pipe a couple of short spikes in the centre of the flower.

4. Pipe small yellow dots at the tip of each spike, again using a piping bag with a small hole at the tip.

5. Repeat the same process and pipe more flowers. To give volume, pipe a small blob of buttercream underneath each blossom.

Lotus

A symbol of purity, these lovely aquatic flowers emerge from water on long stems to bloom with exquisite beauty. Often mistaken for a water lily — on closer inspection the two plants are quite different.

To create this flower...

- Colours: for the petals, pink (Sugarflair Baby Pink (Pastel) plus Melon); for the centre, yellow (Sugarflair Melon plus Autumn Leaf)
- Wilton Leaf Nozzle 366
- Piping bags

1. Pipe a guide circle to determine how big your flower will be, then begin to pipe your petals.

2. Hold the nozzle at a 20 degree angle with one of the points touching the circle. Pipe a petal using the leaf technique (see Basic Petal Strokes). Repeat to pipe a ring of petals close together.

3. Pipe another row of petals that touch your first ring, and that are slightly shorter and at a steeper angle.

4. Depending on how big you want the flower to be, you may pipe another layer of petals making sure that they decrease in size and increase in angle.

5. Using your yellow buttercream and a piping bag with a small hole at the tip, pipe some short spikes in the centre.

TIP
To create a lovely blend of colours for the petals, use the marbled technique (see Filling a Piping Bag, Marbled Effect).

Cosmos

Similar to a daisy, cosmos is easy to grow in the garden even if you don't pay it much attention. The pretty flowerheads have long stems making them great for flower arrangements.

To create this flower...

- Colours: for the petals, light pink and dark pink (Sugarflair Light Claret and Dark Claret) for a two-tone effect; for the centre, yellow (Sugarflair Melon plus Autumn Leaf)
- Wilton Petal Nozzle 103
- Piping bags

1. Pipe a guide circle and fill a piping bag with both shades of pink (see Two-tone Effect). With the wide end of the nozzle touching the circle, hold the bag at a 20 to 30 degree angle.

2. Pipe a fan-shaped petal (see Basic Petal Strokes) using your two-tone colour, the dark pink being the stripe colour.

3. Repeat the same process and pipe a couple of petals around the guide circle. Make sure that there are no gaps between each one.

4. Using yellow buttercream in a piping bag with small hole at the tip, pipe some dots in the centre and build up to create a slight dome.

5. Repeat the same process and pipe more flowers. To give volume, pipe a small blob of buttercream underneath.

Protea

The size of a protea flower is impressive. It has a thick stem topped with clusters of pink flowers, which are arranged into a big flower head with large colourful bracts surrounding it.

To create this flower...

- Colours: for the petals, pink and dark pink (Sugarflair Light Claret and Dark Claret) for a two-tone effect; for the centre, pink (Sugarflair Pink), yellow (Sugarflair Melon plus Autumn Leaf) and green (Sugarflair Gooseberry)
- PME Petal Nozzle 58R
- Piping bags

1. Pipe a small guide circle then, using the pink and dark pink (see Two-tone Effect) and the petal nozzle, pipe a ring of medium-length pulled petals (see Basic Petal Strokes).

2. Pipe a mound of untinted buttercream in the circle with a raised pointed tip at the centre.

3. Using your light pink buttercream in a piping bag with a small hole at the tip, pipe lines all around the centre, starting a few millimetres (1/16in) from the bottom and ending at the tip.

4. Next, using yellow buttercream in a piping bag with a small hole at the tip, pipe shorter lines around the centre starting from the base and ending about halfway up.

5. Using green buttercream in a piping bag with a small hole at the tip, pipe short spikes that start from the bottom of the flower centre and flare outwards. Pipe a second layer.

TIP
For the centre you can use a piece of sponge cake or a balled-up cake instead of piping a big mound of buttercream.

Chrysanthemum

There is a wide variety of shapes and sizes in the chrysanthemum family, and these flowers can be daisy-like, spoon-shaped, spider-like, button-shaped or globe shaped. Ours is an elaborate daisy shape – a real classic!

To create this flower...

- Colours: for the petals, pink (Sugarflair Claret); for the centre, dark pink (Sugarflair Dark Claret) and yellow (Sugarflair Melon plus Autumn Leaf)
- Wilton Nozzle 81
- Piping bags

1. Pipe a guide circle and position the nozzle at a 20 to 30 degree angle with the curved end down, touching your circle. Pipe a layer of pulled petals (see Basic Petal Strokes) of about 0.5cm (¼in).

2. Repeat to pipe two or more layers of petals making sure that they are close to the first layer, and that the length decreases but the angle increases in steepness.

3. Using dark pink buttercream and a piping bag with a small hole at the tip, pipe short spikes around the centre.

4. Repeat, using yellow buttercream, in the very centre of the flower.

5. When buttercream of the petals has crusted, use a cocktail stick (toothpick) to smooth the edge of each one.

Carnation

Popular in corsages and bouquets because of their long life span, carnations also make good potted plants because of their long blooming season. They are naturally bright in colour and possess a subtle sweet smell.

To create this flower...

- Colours: pale pink (Sugarflair Baby Pink (Pastel)) and dark pink (Sugarflair Dark Claret) for a two-tone effect
- Wilton Petal Nozzle 104
- Piping bags

1. Using a piping bag with small hole cut in the tip, pipe a circle for your guide. Fill a piping bag with both shades of pink (see Two-tone Effect).

2. With the nozzle at 20 to 30 degree angle, the wider end touching the surface, pipe a ring of ruffle petals (see Basic Petal Strokes) following the guide.

3. Repeat the same process and pipe another layer of petals on top of the first at a steeper angle.

4. Repeat the same process to create several layers of petals until you have filled the middle and the flower makes a rounded dome shape.

TIP

To create a Carnation that is facing sideways, pipe your first layer of petals following a half circle shape. Succeeding petals should overlap the previous ones as the length decreases. You may also use different colours to give a variation, as well as different sizes of nozzles, such as Wilton Petal 103, 124, 125 or 126.

Rhododendron

Large trusses of bell-shaped flowers are the characteristic blooms of the rhododendron. A shrub can bear up to 20 blossoms in a single truss, making it a sight to behold when it is in full bloom.

To create this flower...

- Colours: for the petals, pink (Sugarflair Claret); for the centre, red (Sugarflair Red)
- Wilton Petal Nozzle 104
- Piping bags

1. Position the nozzle at a 20 to 30 degree angle and pipe a fan-shaped petal (see Basic Petal Strokes) in pink.

2. Repeat the same process and pipe four or five more petals from a central point.

3. Using your red buttercream in a piping bag with small hole cut at the tip, pipe a few short lines in the centre.

4. Using the same piping bag, pipe some small dots in the centre.

5. Pipe a couple more flowers to make a cluster. Pipe a blob underneath each flower to give volume, and see Leaves if you wish to add foliage.

Peony

Showy peonies produce large, often fragrant flowers, and make a fine addition to the garden because of their dashing looks. These flowers range from white through pink and red to the darkest purple.

To create this flower...

- Colours: for the petals, pale pink (Sugarflair Baby Pink (Pastel)) and dark pink (Sugarflair Claret); for the centre, yellow (Sugarflair Melon plus Autumn Leaf) and green (Sugarflair Gooseberry)
- Wilton Petal Nozzles 104 and 126
- Flower nail
- Piping bags

1. Pipe a mound of buttercream on the flower nail, and using a piping bag with a small hole at the tip, pipe four small green bean shapes in the centre.

2. Using yellow buttercream in a piping bag with a small hole at the tip, pipe short spikes in the centre, but do not cover the green bean shapes.

3. With the Wilton 104 Nozzle against the mound at a 90 degree angle, pipe a medium length upright curved petal (see Basic Petal Strokes) in pale pink. Repeat to pipe petals that overlap as shown.

4. Pipe two or three rounds of petals in the same way.

5. Using the Wilton 126 nozzle with dark pink buttercream, repeat the same process to pipe more petals around until you are happy with the flower size.

TIP
You may find parts of the mound show underneath the peony, cover up by piping leaves at the base of the flower (see Leaves).

Sweet Pea

Cottage garden favourites, sweet peas are climbing plants that bear clusters of flowers that are lightly sweet scented. They look like butterflies in popular colours of pink, white, and light blue.

To create this flower...

- Colours: for the petals, pink (Sugarflair Pink); for the centre, light green (Sugarflair Gooseberry)
- Wilton Petal Nozzle 103
- Piping bags

1. Hold the piping bag at a 20 to 30 degree angle with the narrow end of the nozzle in a 7 o'clock position and pipe a fan-shaped petal (see Basic Petal Strokes).

2. Pipe another fan-shaped petal opposite the first with no gap between them.

3. Pipe two small upright petals (see Basic Petal Strokes) in a V-shape.

4. Pipe the centre of the flower using light green buttercream in a piping bag with a small hole in the tip.

5. Repeat the same process and pipe more flowers. To give volume, pipe a small blob of buttercream underneath.

TIP
Sweet peas are good filler flowers that you can pipe directly onto the top or side of a cake. If you wish to create a varied posy, common colours of this flower are light shades of blue, pink, cream, lavender, red and white.

Bouvardia

Sometimes known as the daphne flower, bouvardia can have single or double star-like blooms that open from tubular necks. These flowers are lightly scented and are fringed with leaves.

To create this flower...

- Colours: for the petals, pink (Sugarflair Pink); for the centre, dark pink (Sugarflair Claret plus Ruby Red)
- PME Petal Nozzle 32R
- Piping bags

1. Hold the piping bag and nozzle at a 20 degree angle and pipe five simple petals (see Basic Petal Strokes) that join together at a common centre.

2. Using your dark pink buttercream in a piping bag with a small hole at the tip, pipe a small circle in the centre.

3. Repeat the same process and pipe more flowers. To give volume, pipe a small blob of buttercream underneath each flower.

4. Pipe single simple petals randomly to make the small buds.

5. Use the dark pink buttercream to pipe the stems for the buds.

Boronia

This woodland shrub is a favourite for flower arrangements as boronia flowers have a long life even after cutting. The delightful four-petalled flowers are scented, and borne in clusters on long stems.

To create this flower...

- Colours: for the petals, magenta (Sugarflair Claret); for the centre, yellow (Sugarflair Melon plus Autumn Leaf)
- PME Petal Nozzle 58R
- Piping bags

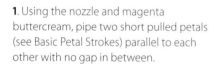

1. Using the nozzle and magenta buttercream, pipe two short pulled petals (see Basic Petal Strokes) parallel to each other with no gap in between.

2. Pipe two more short pulled petals on top of the bottom petals but pull the piping bag outwards, towards the tip to give a slightly curved look to the petals.

3. Pipe a couple more flowers to create a cluster, then pipe short spikes in the centre of each flower using yellow buttercream in a piping bag with a small hole at the tip.

TIP
Make sure you wait for the buttercream to crust before you use a toothpick to manipulate the petals otherwise they will be too sticky.

4. When the petals have crusted, use a cocktail stick (toothpick) to smooth the edge of each one and to curl them further, if need be.

Freesia

Beautiful bell-shaped blooms, strongly scented and in a wonderful range of colours, freesias are one of the most popular springtime flowers. The single, or double flowers, grow along one side of the stem, in groups of up to ten.

To create this flower...

- Colours: for the petals, magenta (Sugarflair Claret) and untinted buttercream for a two-tone effect; for the centre, yellow (Sugarflair Melon plus Autumn Leaf); for the stems, green (Sugarflair Gooseberry)
- Wilton Petal Nozzle 103
- Piping bags

1. Using the green buttercream in a piping bag with a small hole at the tip, pipe your stems.

2. Pipe simple petals (see Basic Petal Strokes) in magenta and untinted buttercream (see Two-tone Effect), at the tip of the stem and then each side of it.

3. Using your green tinted buttercream, pipe the calyx and connecting stems.

4. Starting at the base, pipe about three or four small fan-shaped petals (see Basic Petal Strokes) to form a small flower.

5. Repeat the same process and pipe several small flowers, in two columns, up the sides of the stem.

6. Pipe four short yellow spikes, using a piping bag with a small hole at the tip, in the centre of each flower. Then pipe a green dot in the centre of the spikes.

Camellia

The camellia is a very beautiful flower that is famous for its magnificent display of large blooms in spring. Flowers can be single or double and come in various eye-catching colours.

To create this flower...

- Colours: for the petals, magenta (Sugarflair Claret); for the centre, yellow (Sugarflair Melon plus Autumn Leaf)
- Wilton Petal Nozzle 104
- Piping bags

1. Pipe a guide circle as big you want the flower to be and position your nozzle at a 20 to 30 degree angle with the wide end of nozzle touching the guide circle.

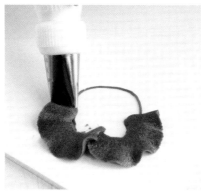

2. Pipe a ring of long curved petals (see Basic Petal Strokes) using magenta buttercream and the nozzle, to form the first layer of petals.

3. Repeat the same process and pipe another layer of petals at a 30 to 40 degree angle, making them slightly shorter than the petals in the first layer.

4. Depending on how big your flower is, you may need to pipe another layer of petals, making sure that the angle increases but length decreases.

5. Using the yellow buttercream in a piping bag with a small hole at the tip, pipe short spikes in the centre.

Love Lies Bleeding

Also known as amaranthus, this is a showy, exotic looking plant that adds an excellent dramatic accent to any display, with flowers that cascade to the ground from the top of branching stems.

To create this flower...

- Colours: for the petals, magenta (Sugarflair Dark Claret); for the leaves, green (Sugarflair Gooseberry)
- PME Nozzle 42 and Wilton Leaf Nozzle 352
- Piping bags

1. Pipe some guidelines to help with positioning.

2. With the magenta buttercream and the PME Nozzle 42, held at a 90 degree angle, gently squeeze the piping bag with even pressure to create a star.

3. Repeat to pipe a series of stars that resemble a long wavy teardrop. Make the base of the flower bulge, and create a pointed tip by pulling piping bag away.

4. Repeat steps 2 to 3 to pipe more wavy teardrop shapes, making some overlap the others.

5. Pipe small leaves in green using the Wilton 352 Leaf Nozzle.

Dahlia

Considered one of the most beautiful garden flowers, dahlia blooms consist of many delicate petals in mesmerising concentric circles, and are perfect in almost any garden location.

To create this flower...

- Colours: for the petals, magenta (Sugarflair Claret)
- Wilton Nozzle 81
- Piping bags

1. Pipe a mound of buttercream (or use a cake ball) by cutting the tip off a piping bag.

2. Holding the nozzle horizontally, with the curve pointing downwards, squeeze evenly and gently pull away to create a short pulled petal (see Basic Petal Strokes) about 1cm (½in) long. Repeat to create one layer of petals.

3. Repeat the same process and pipe more layers of petals, keeping them the same length but increasing the steepness of the angle with each layer.

4. When the buttercream has crusted use a cocktail stick (toothpick) to smooth the edge of the petals.

Ranunculus

With layers of tissue paper-thin petals, these brilliantly coloured blooms make long-lasting cut flowers. The large flowers of ranunculus are an exceptional sight when planted in large swathes.

To create this flower...

- Colours: for the petals, very light green (Sugarflair Light Gooseberry) and dark pink (Sugarflair Claret); for the centre, green (Sugarflair Spruce Green)
- Wilton Petal Nozzles 104 and 126
- Flower nail
- Piping bags

1. Pipe a mound of buttercream onto your flower nail for the base. Then pipe a small mound in the centre, using green buttercream and a piping bag with a medium sized hole at the tip.

2. Hold the Petal Nozzle 104 against the mound, slightly tilted to the centre, and pipe a medium-length upright curved petal (see Basic Petal Strokes) with very light green buttercream.

3. Repeat the same process making each subsequent petal start a little past the middle of the previous one.

4. Using dark pink buttercream and the 104 Nozzle, repeat the same process and pipe even longer petals outside the light green ones.

5. Swap to the Wilton Petal Nozzle 126, and with dark pink, repeat the same process to pipe petals around the flower until you are happy with the size.

TIP
Keep the height of all the petals nice and low, otherwise your Ranunculus will look more like a rose.

Petunia

Common garden favourites, petunias are nonetheless lovely in their many varieties. Most are sweetly fragrant, and the petals may be a single colour only or mixed to add contrast and definition to the flower.

To create this flower...

- Colours: for the petals, light pink (Sugarflair Claret) and magenta (Sugarflair Dark Claret) for a two-tone effect; for the stem and calyx, green (Sugarflair Gooseberry)
- Wilton Petal Nozzle 103
- Piping bags

1. Using light pink and magenta buttercream (see Blended Two-tone Effect), hold your nozzle at a 20 to 30 degree angle and pipe a small fan-shaped petal (see Basic Petal Strokes).

2. Repeat the same process and pipe three or four more petals that start from the middle of each previous petal, making a tight ring.

3. Using light pink buttercream in a piping bag with a small hole at the tip, pipe a few spikes in the centre.

TIP
There are several colour variations for this flower, such as red, burgundy, blue, white and yellow and a few two-tone varieties. Use two buttercream colours in the same piping bag, and blend them slightly (see Blended Two-tone Effect) to give a rather beautiful multi-coloured petal.

4. To pipe another flower, pipe a blob of buttercream underneath and repeat the same process.

Verbena

Perfect for hanging baskets, verbena are easy going plants that will bloom reliably even on the hottest day of the year. The flowers bloom in clusters and the plants are available in a variety of sizes and colours.

To create this flower...

- Colours: for the petals, magenta (Sugarflair Claret); for the centre, pink (Sugarflair Claret)
- PME Petal Nozzle 58R
- Piping bags

1. Using the nozzle and the magenta buttercream, hold the piping bag at a 20 to 30 degree angle and pipe a heart-shaped petal (see Basic Petal Strokes).

2. Repeat the same process and pipe three more heart-shaped petals from a single central point.

3. Using pink buttercream in a piping bag with a small hole at the tip, pipe a small dot in the centre of the flower.

TIP
These flowers work really well when grouped together. Make sure that you pipe the flowers close to each other to make a lovely bunch.

4. To pipe another flower, pipe a blob of buttercream underneath and repeat the same process.

Cockscomb

A plant of many names, cockscomb flowers are also known as Wool Flowers or Brain Celosia. The names derive from the fluffy appearance of the flowers and their resemblance to a highly coloured brain or a rooster's comb.

To create this flower...

- Colours: for the petals: dark pink (Sugarflair Claret plus Sugarflair Orange)
- Wilton Petal Nozzle 150
- Piping bags

1. Pipe a circle for a positional guide.

2. With the nozzle at a 20 to 30 degree angle and the wider end of the slit touching the surface, pipe a row of ruffle petals (see Basic Petal Strokes) following the guide circle.

3. Repeat the same process and pipe another layer of petals at a steeper angle.

4. Repeat the same process to create several layers of petals until you fill the middle and the petals create a dome shape.

Thistle

Common flowers, which are found in a range of dark pinks, blues and purples, thistles are the national flower of Scotland. Their leaves are alternately arranged, lobed and armed with stiff spikes.

To create this flower...

- Colours: for the petals, dark pink (Sugarflair Claret); for the calyx, green (Sugarflair Gooseberry)
- PME Leaf Nozzle ST50
- Piping bags

1. Pipe a fan-shaped guide in dark pink to help with the positioning of the petals.

2. Using dark pink buttercream in a piping bag with a small hole at the tip, pipe long spikes following your guide. Repeat to create another layer, with no gaps.

3. Repeat the same process and pipe more layers, making sure that the spikes are close to the layer below and that the angle of the spikes gradually increases.

4. Pipe a few layers of leaf technique petals (see Basic Petal Strokes) for the calyx using green buttercream and the leaf nozzle.

Amaryllis

The amaryllis has long, narrow leaves and large trumpet-like flowers, comprising of six petals. It comes in a variety of colours – usually a combination of shades of pink and red with white.

To create this flower...

- Colours: for the petals light red (Sugarflair Ruby Red plus Claret) and untinted buttercream for a two-tone effect; for the centre, green (Sugarflair Gooseberry), white (Sugarflair Super White) and yellow (Sugarflair Melon plus Autumn Leaf)
- Wilton Petal Nozzle 104
- Piping bags

1. Prepare the dark pink and untinted buttercream (see Blended Two-tone Effect), and pipe a dot for the start, one for the tip and one for the end of the first petal, creating a Y-shaped guide.

2. Hold your piping bag at a 20 to 30 degree angle and pipe a rounded two-stroke petal (see Basic Petal Strokes), following your marks.

3. Repeat steps 1 and 2 to make three petals.

4. Pipe three more rounded two-stroke petals between the first three petals.

5. Using your light green buttercream in a piping bag with a small hole at the tip, pipe the centre.

6. Using untinted buttercream, pipe short spikes all going in one direction. Then in yellow, pipe a short line across the tip of each white spike.

Anemone

These are large and versatile flowers that come in a range of lively colours. The saucer-shaped blooms usually appear in clusters and are found naturally in woodland habitats.

To create this flower...

- Colours: for the petals, red (Sugarflair Red); for the centre, white (Sugarflair Super White) and black (Sugarflair Black Extra)
- Wilton Petal Nozzle 104
- Piping bags

1. Pipe a circle as a guide for the size of your flower, and position your nozzle at a 20 to 30 degree angle with the wide end of nozzle touching the guide circle.

2. Pipe a couple of long curved petals (see Basic Petal Strokes) to form the first layer of petals.

3. Repeat the same process and pipe another layer of petals at a 30 to 40 degree angle and slightly shorter in length than the first.

4. Cover the centre with white buttercream, using a piping bag with a small hole at the tip.

5. Using black buttercream in a piping bag with a small hole at the tip, pipe short spikes in the centre.

Anthurium

Sometimes known as the flamingo flower, anthuriums are grown for their glossy heart-shaped 'spathes' with contrasting central 'spadix', which contains the true flowers. They are also known for their ornamental leaves.

To create this flower...

- Colours: for the petals, dark red (Sugarflair Red plus Black); for the centre, white (Sugarflair Super White) and yellow (Sugarflair Melon plus Autumn Leaf)
- Wilton Petal Nozzle 126
- Flower nail (optional)
- Piping bags

1. Using the flower nail, or piping directly onto a cupcake, and the dark red buttercream, hold the nozzle in a 6 o'clock position, at a 5 to 10 degree angle.

2. Squeeze with even pressure and turn the flower nail clockwise to make the left side of the petal, giving it a wider base.

3. Complete the left side by squeezing the piping bag with even pressure, and pulling up to the desired length.

4. You may stop at the tip, or keep going and turn the nozzle to the right, pulling down to make the right side. Curve round at the base to form a heart shape.

5. Pipe the white centre, using a bag with a hole at the tip. Apply firm pressure at the base and gently release towards the tip. Complete the tip in yellow.

6. Cover the centre with tight dots using white and yellow buttercream in piping bags with a small hole at the tip.

Rose

A classic favourite and by far the most popular flower with more than a hundred varieties, the rose is a symbol of love. A single bloom on a cupcake or a cake says it all.

To create this flower...

- Colours: for the petals, dark red (Sugarflair Red plus Black); for the stem and calyx, green (Sugarflair Gooseberry)
- Wilton Petal Nozzle 104
- Flower nail
- Piping bags

1. Position the nozzle flat against the flower nail and squeeze the piping bag as you turn the nail to create a base.

2. Hold the nozzle vertically, with the wide end touching the surface, slightly tilted inward so your bud will have only a small opening. Squeeze the piping bag as you turn the flower nail clockwise until you make both ends meet.

3. While the nozzle is still slightly tilted inwards, turn the flower nail and pipe an upright curved petal (see Basic Petal Strokes) in an arch-shape around the bud, slightly pushing against the bud so there are no gaps and it will not collapse.

4. Each subsequent petal should begin slightly past the middle of the previous one and overlap it. Pipe about two to four short petals.

5. After creating the bud with few petals around it, hold the nozzle vertically and pipe four to five slightly longer and higher arched upright curved petals.

6. When piping the last few petals, tilt the nozzle slightly outwards and make the arches longer instead of higher. Pipe about four to five outer petals.

Poinsettia

Ever popular at Christmas time, poinsettias have brightly coloured bracts, often mistaken as petals, that are actually the upper leaves of the plant. The true flowers grow modestly in small central clusters.

To create this flower...

- Colours: for the petals, red (Sugarflair Red plus Orange); for the centre, yellow (Sugarflair Melon plus Autumn Leaf)
- Wilton Leaf Nozzle 366
- Piping bags

1. Pipe a guide circle to determine the starting point of your petals.

2. With the nozzle flat on the surface, the tip touching the circle, pipe a leaf technique petal (see Basic Petal Strokes). Turn slightly as you release the pressure.

3. When you reach the desired length, stop squeezing and pull the nozzle abruptly.

4. Repeat the same process and pipe a total of six petals for the first layer.

5. Repeat steps 2 to 4 and pipe another layer of six petals that are slightly shorter than the first. Ideally pipe in between the petals of the first layer.

6. Using your yellow buttercream in a piping bag with a medium hole cut at the tip, pipe about six to eight big dots for the centre.

Hibiscus

These showy flowers have quite a tropical appearance. Hibiscus blossoms have beautifully coloured centres that protrude dramatically from the horn of the flower.

To create this flower...

- Colours: for the petals and centre spikes, red (Sugarflair Red plus Orange); for the centre, deep orange (more Sugarflair Red plus a little Orange) and yellow (Sugarfliar Melon plus Autumn Leaf)
- Wilton Petal Nozzle 104
- Piping bags

1. Pipe guide marks to help you position the five petals.

2. Using red buttercream and holding the piping bag at the starting point, at a 20 to 30 degree angle, pipe a long curved two-stroke petal (see Basic Petal Strokes).

3. Repeat the same process and pipe a total of five petals.

4. Using deep orange buttercream, pipe the centre by squeezing firmly on a piping bag with a medium hole cut at the tip and gradually pull upwards.

5. Pipe small dots around the tip of the centre using yellow buttercream in a piping bag with a small hole cut at the tip.

6. Pipe about two to four short spikes from the tip of the centre using red buttercream in a piping bag with a small hole cut at the tip.

Blanket Flower

Gaillardia or blanket flowers are rich-coloured daisy-like flowers. They often come in various shades of red and yellow. The petals of some are frilled, while others have a unique tubular shape.

To create this flower...

- Colours: for the petals, red (Sugarflair Red) and yellow (Sugarflair Melon) for a two-tone effect; for the centre, green (Sugarflair Gooseberry) and red (Sugarflair Ruby Red)
- Wilton Petal Nozzle 104
- Piping bags

1. Pipe a guide circle and position your nozzle touching the circle at a 20 to 30 degree angle. Using red and yellow buttercream (see Two-tone Effect), pipe an up-down petal (see Basic Petal Strokes) about 1cm (½in) long.

2. Repeat the same process and pipe petals all the way around the guide circle.

3. Build up small piped dots in the centre of the flower using green buttercream in a piping bag with a small hole in the tip.

TIP
When piping the centre of your Blanket Flower, you can pipe spikes or dots around the green centre – both will look equally authentic!

4. Pipe two or three layers of short spikes around the green centre using red buttercream.

5. Repeat steps 1 to 4 and pipe a few more flowers. Piping them close to each other creates a stunning effect.

Poppy

Found in many colours, including red, poppies are one of the most popular flowering plants. The paper-like petals unfurl from their crumpled beginnings in the bud to come to full showy bloom.

To create this flower...

- Colours: for the petals, red (Sugarflair Red plus Black); for the centre, green (Sugarflair Gooseberry) and black (Sugarflair Black)
- Wilton Petal Nozzle 126
- Piping bags

1. Start to pipe the left-hand petal by holding the piping bag at a 20 to 30 degree angle and piping a long curved petal (see Basic Petal Strokes).

2. Pipe another long curved petal of the same size opposite the first.

3. Pipe a slightly shorter curved petal in between the first two petals at a steeper angle. Repeat on the other side.

4. Pipe a small blob in the centre using green buttercream in a piping bag with a small hole cut at the tip. Then cover with spikes running from the bottom and all meeting up at the tip.

5. Using black buttercream in a piping bag with a small hole at the tip, pipe a few layers of short spikes around the green centre.

Zinnia

These long-lasting flowers come in bright colours with large mixed blooms. Zinnias have bright, individual daisy-like flowerheads on a single stem.

To create this flower...

- Colours: for the petals, red (Sugarflair Red plus Orange); for the centre, brown (Sugarflair Gooseberry plus Brown), red (Sugarflair Ruby Red) and yellow (Sugarflair Melon plus Autumn Leaf)
- Wilton Nozzle 81
- Piping bags

1. Pipe a mound of buttercream (or use a cake ball) using a simple round nozzle or just cut the tip of the piping bag.

2. Hold the nozzle horizontally with the curve downwards, squeeze evenly and gently pull away to create a petal about 0.5cm (¼in) long. Repeat to create a layer of petals around the base of the mound.

3. Repeat the same process and pipe a few more layers of petals, keeping the same length but increasing the angle with each layer.

4. Pipe a mound of dots in the centre using brown buttercream in a piping bag with a small hole in the tip.

5. Pipe a few very short red spikes in the middle of the brown mound and pipe short yellow spikes around them.

6. Use a cocktail stick (toothpick) to smooth the edges of the petals once the buttercream has crusted.

Trillium

The unusual flower of the trillium has three petals and rises above trios of leaf-like bracts. As the name suggests, the trillium does everything in threes!

To create this flower...

- Colours: for the petals, dark red (Sugarflair Red plus Black); for the centre, yellow (Sugarflair Melon plus Autumn Leaf)
- Wilton Petal Nozzle 104
- Piping bags

1. Pipe guide marks to help position the three petals.

2. Hold the piping bag at a 20 to 30 degree angle and pipe a non-ruffled two-stroke petal (see Basic Petal Strokes).

3. Repeat the same process and pipe a total of three petals of equal length and without gaps in between.

4. Use the yellow buttercream in a piping bag with a medium hole at the tip to pipe a couple of thick but short spikes in the centre of the flower.

TIP
The other popular colour of Trillium is white, and for another variation you can also use a big Wilton 366 Leaf Nozzle to pipe this flower. Make sure that you always pipe the leaves or sepals first before you pipe the main petals on top.

Tiger Lily

The tiger lily is a large fiery flower, with dark spots on its petals and up to six prominent stamens. These characteristics make it a bright and showy statement in gardens and flower arrangements alike.

To create this flower...

- Colours: for the petals, orange-red (Sugarflair Orange plus Red); for the centre, red (Sugarflair Red); for the dots, violet (Sugarflair Grape Violet)
- Wilton Petal Nozzle 104
- Piping bags

1. Pipe a Y-shape guide mark for your first three petals.

2. Holding your piping bag at a 20 to 30 degree angle, and using the nozzle and the orange-red buttercream, pipe three rounded two-stroke petals (see Basic Petal Strokes), following your marks.

3. Pipe three more rounded two-stroke petals in between the first three petals.

4. Using red buttercream in a piping bag with a small hole at the tip, pipe a few short lines coming from the centre.

5. Use violet buttercream in a piping bag with a small hole at the tip to pipe short lines perpendicular to the tips of the red lines to make the stamens.

6. Randomly pipe very small dots around each petal using the violet buttercream.

Gerber Daisy

With layers of thin petals, gerber daisy blooms are large with yellowish central disks surrounded by colourful rays. They are said to convey happiness making them a popular choice on many occasions.

To create this flower...

- Colours: for the petals, orange-red (Sugarflair Orange plus Red); for the centre, brown (Sugarflair Gooseberry plus Brown) and orange (Sugarflair Orange)
- Wilton Petal Nozzle 81
- Piping bags

1. Pipe a guide circle to determine the position of your petals.

2. Hold the nozzle with the curved end down, flat to the surface. Pipe a pulled petal (see Basic Petal Strokes) of about 2cm (1in). Pipe a layer of petals, all the same length, around the guide circle.

3. Repeat the same process and pipe another layer of petals, which are slightly shorter than the first. Ideally, pipe in between the first layer of petals.

4. Pipe very short spikes in the centre using brown buttercream in a piping bag with a small hole at the tip.

5. Using orange buttercream in a bag with a small hole at the tip, pipe about three layers of spikes in decreasing length starting from the outermost row and working towards the centre.

6. When the petals are crusted, use a cocktail stick to smooth the edge of each petal.

Clementine

These bright orange flowers have fuzzy violet-purple filament hairs in the centre, with large rippled green leaves that form tidy rosettes below. Their catchy look make them perfect in garden borders.

To create this flower...

- Colours: for the petals, orange (Sugarflair Orange); for the stem, green (Sugarflair Gooseberry); for the buds and centre, violet (Sugarflair Grape Violet) and red (Sugarflair Red)
- Wilton Petal Nozzle 58R
- Piping bags

1. Using green buttercream in a piping bag with a small hole at the tip, pipe your stem to the desired length. Then, starting at the tip, pipe small overlapping buds using fairly firm pressure.

2. Repeat the same process to pipe a few more buds using violet buttercream.

3. Start piping the flowers at the base of the stem using the nozzle and orange buttercream. Position the first petal on one side of the stem. Each flower will have at least five petals.

4. Repeat the same process and pipe more flowers making sure that they are close together without gaps, and overlapping.

5. Use violet buttercream to pipe about three or four short spikes in the flower centres.

6. Use red buttercream to pipe short lines perpendicular to the tip of the violet lines to finish the flower centres.

Marigold

Although marigolds come in different colours, orange and yellow are the most common. The flowers are made up of multiple layers of overlapping petals, which get smaller and smaller as they get closer to the centre.

To create this flower...

- Colours: for the petals, orange (Sugarflair Orange plus a hint of Melon); for the calyx, green (Sugarflair Gooseberry)
- Wilton Petal Nozzle 58R
- Piping bags

1. For a Marigold facing sideways, pipe a semi-circle as a guide. Position your nozzle at a 20 to 30 degree angle with the wide end touching your guide and pipe a simple petal (see Basic Petal Strokes).

2. Pipe layers of simple petals, ensuring that they are close together, increasing the angle but decreasing the number of petals as you pipe towards the base.

3. Use the green buttercream in a piping bag with a small hole at the tip to pipe the calyx.

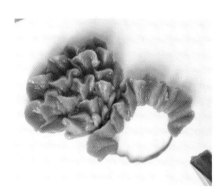

4. For a flat Marigold, pipe a full circle as your guide. Position your nozzle at a 20 to 30 degree angle, with the wide end touching your circle. Pipe a layer of ruffled petals (see Basic Flower Strokes).

5. Repeat the same process and pipe few more layers of ruffled petals.

6. For the top-most petals, pipe a couple of upright petals (see Basic Flower Strokes) to finish the flower.

Tiki Torch

A variety of echinacea, tiki torch has large bright pumpkin-orange flowers, which feature drooping petals and rounded, reddish-brown centre cones. They are favourites for cut flowers.

To create this flower...

- Colours: for the petals, orange (Sugarflair Orange plus Red); for the stem and calyx, green (Sugarflair Gooseberry plus Dark Brown)
- Wilton Petal Nozzle 104
- Piping bags

1. Pipe a circle as a guide.

2. Hold the nozzle flat to the surface, with the wide end of the nozzle touching the guide circle. Then pipe an up-down petal (see Basic Petal Strokes) in orange buttercream.

3. Repeat to pipe more petals making sure that each one starts and ends at your guide circle.

4. Using brown buttercream in a piping bag with a medium-sized hole at the tip, pipe a mound in the centre, then pipe short spikes to cover the centre cone.

5. To pipe another flower, pipe a blob of buttercream underneath and repeat the same process.

Begonia

Ranging from trailing to sturdy upright plants, begonias are known for their large, waxy-petalled flowers, in bright showy colours. These may be plain, ruffled and even bi-coloured.

To create this flower...

- Colours: for the petals, orange (Sugarflair Orange)
- Wilton Petal Nozzle 104
- Flower nail (optional)
- Piping bags

1. Pipe a mound of buttercream for the base, either straight on a cupcake or on a flower nail. Then hold the nozzle vertically and squeezing the piping bag, turn counter-clockwise to create a bud.

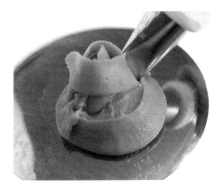

2. With the nozzle tilted slightly inwards, pipe an arch-shaped upright petal (see Basic Petal Strokes) as you turn. It should go around the bud and be pushed against it. Pipe two to four short petals.

3. Turn the nozzle straight, then pipe a couple of slightly longer and higher 'arches'. Continue to build up the flower by piping arch-shaped petals, increasing the size as the flower becomes bigger.

4. Repeat the same process and pipe more petals.

5. If it is becoming difficult to pipe in the same direction, you can pipe the petals in a clockwise direction.

TIP

Each arched petal that you pipe around the bud should begin just past the centre of the previous one and overlap it. They should be pressed against the bud so they do not collapse.

Bush Lily

These tall-stemmed flowers vary in shape from an open cup to a narrow hanging tube. Ours is a vivid orange rounded cluster of blooms, but you could vary it to yellow or red orange.

To create this flower...

- Colours: for the petals, orange (Sugarflair Orange) and yellow (Sugarflair Melon) for a two-tone effect; for the centre, yellow (Sugarflair Melon)
- Wilton Petal Nozzle 103
- Piping bags

1. Using both orange and yellow buttercream in your piping bag (see Two-tone Effect) and the nozzle, hold the bag at a 20 to 30 degree angle ready to pipe your first petal.

2. Pipe five small simple petals (see Basic Petal Strokes) that meet in the centre.

3. Repeat the same process and pipe more flowers, making sure that there are few gaps by slightly overlapping them as much as possible.

4. Using yellow buttercream in a piping bag with a small hole at the tip, pipe short spikes in the centre of each of the flowers.

TIP
If you want to include leaves, make sure that you pipe these before piping the flowers. To increase the height of the flower, you can either pipe a mound of buttercream or use a small piece of cake to elevate the flower.

Hypericum Berries

These clusters of ornamental berries come in orange, purple, pink and white. They are easy to grow and add unique character and texture to flower arrangements.

To create this flower...

- Colours: for the berries, orange (Sugarflair Orange plus Gooseberry) and dark orange (Sugarflair Orange and Red); for the leaves, green (Sugarflair Gooseberry) for the stem, dark brown (Sugarflair Dark Brown)
- PME Leaf Nozzle ST50
- Piping bags

1. Using your dark brown buttercream in a piping bag with a small hole at the tip, pipe the stems.

2. With orange buttercream in a piping bag with a small hole at the tip, hold the bag at a 70 to 80 degree angle and pipe a berry, squeezing firmly to create a rounded blob.

3. Pipe more berries randomly around the stems.

4. Using your small leaf nozzle, pipe two or three leaves per berry.

5. Pipe a dot of dark orange buttercream at the tip of each berry using a piping bag with a small hole at the tip.

Alstroemeria

Featuring delicate, trumpet-shaped flowers on the end of short stalks, alstroemeria is a symmetrical flower with three sepals and three patterned petals, which have characteristic dark speckles.

To create this flower...

- Colours: for the petals, orange and light orange (Sugarflair Orange); for the centre, red (Sugarflair Red) and violet (Sugarflair Grape Violet)
- Wilton Petal Nozzle 104 and PME Leaf Nozzle 57R
- Piping bags

1. Pipe a Y-shaped mark to help position your first three petals.

2. Using orange buttercream, hold your Wilton 104 Nozzle at a 20 to 30 degree angle and pipe three simple petals (see Basic Petal Strokes), with the wide end of the nozzle towards the flower centre.

3. Using the light orange buttercream in a piping bag with the PME Leaf Nozzle 57R, pipe three smaller simple petals in between the first three petals.

4. Using the violet buttercream in a piping bag with a small hole at the tip, pipe very small dots randomly on the smaller light orange petals.

5. Pipe short red spikes in the centre of each flower, using a piping bag with a small hole at the tip. Then add short lines perpendicular to the tip of each in violet.

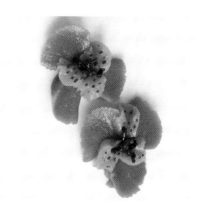

6. Repeat the same process and pipe a few more flowers close to each other.

Anisacanthus

The tubular flowers of anisacanthus usually come in shades of bright orange or red, occasionally yellow. Each long flower has a wide lower lip that falls open to show the inside of the blossom.

To create this flower...

- Colours: for the petals and buds, dark orange (Sugarflair Orange plus Red); for the calyx and stem, green (Sugarflair Gooseberry), for the centre spikes, orange (Sugarflair Orange plus Red) and yellow (Sugarflair Melon)
- PME Petal Nozzle 87R
- Piping bags

1. Using the nozzle and dark orange buttercream, pipe two short pulled petals (see Basic Petal Strokes) parallel to each other with no gap in between. Pipe two more petals on top of the first two.

2. Using the same dark orange buttercream pipe a thick tubular bud by pressing quite firmly on the piping bag.

3. Using orange buttercream in a piping bag with a small hole at the tip, pipe short spikes coming from the centre of the flower.

4. Add yellow dots at the tip of the spikes, using a piping bag with a small hole at the tip. Then pipe the green calyx.

5. Pipe a couple more flowers to create a lovely bunch and pipe some tubular but pointed buds as well, using dark orange buttercream.

6. When the petals have crusted, use a cocktail stick to smooth the edge of each one and to curl them even more if necessary.

Sunflower

Undoubtedly one of the most well-loved flowers, sunflowers always seem to steal the scene. The large flower centre is actually made up of thousands of tiny florets and is surrounded by bright, often yellow, petals.

To create this flower...

- Colours: for the petals, yellow (Sugarflair Melon plus a hint of Autumn Leaf); for the centre, brown (Sugarflair Dark Brown)
- Wilton Leaf Nozzle 352
- Piping bags

1. Pipe a guide circle. Then using the nozzle held at a 20 to 30 degree angle with one of the points touching your guide, pipe a leaf technique petal (see Basic Petal Strokes) in yellow.

2. Repeat the same process to pipe a layer of petals around the guide circle.

3. Pipe another layer of petals at a slightly steeper angle than the first, about 30 to 40 degrees, and make sure that they are close to the first layer to avoid gaps.

4. Finally, using brown buttercream in a piping bag with a small hole at the tip, pipe little dots in the centre of the flower.

TIP
Ideally, when you pipe the second layer, try to pipe the petals in between those of the first layer.

False Dandelion

The flowers of the false dandelion are bright and yellow, similar to a common dandelion. Also known as catsear, the plant has furry leaves that resemble the ear of a cat.

To create this flower...

- Colours: for the petals, yellow and darker yellow (Sugarflair Melon plus Autumn Leaf)
- No nozzle required
- Piping bags

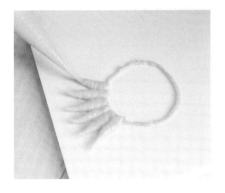

1. Pipe a guide circle. Using the yellow buttercream in a piping bag with a medium hole at the tip, pipe spikes about 1cm (½in) long, starting from the guide circle and working outwards.

2. When you have created a complete circle of petal-spikes, pipe a mound of buttercream in the centre.

3. Pipe more spikes in layers using the same colour but decreasing their length as you move to the top of the mound.

4. Change to a darker shade of yellow buttercream when almost at the top and repeat the same process.

5. Pipe a mound of buttercream close to your first flower and repeat the process to create a second flower.

Gladiolus

The eye-catching gladiolus has strikingly tall upright spikes of six to eight blossoms that open in sequence. These flowers can be used as a full stem to give impact to any arrangement or just as a simple single flower.

To create this flower...

- Colours: for the petals, yellow (Sugarflair Melon); for the centre, red-orange (Sugarflair Orange plus Red) and dark yellow (Sugarflair Melon plus Autumn Leaf)
- PME Petal Nozzle 57R
- Piping bags

1. Using green buttercream in a piping bag with a small hole at the tip, pipe a stem. Starting at the top, use yellow to pipe small fat buds by squeezing firmly on the bag, then connect them to the stem with green.

2. Using the nozzle and yellow buttercream, pipe a fan-shaped petal (see Basic Petal Strokes) on one side of the stem at the bottom, then pipe two or three more to create the first flower. Pipe three or four flowers at the base.

3. Repeat the same process making sure that the flowers decrease in number as you progress up the stem, and that they are tightly packed without gaps, and overlap.

4. Pipe simple petals (see Basic Petal Strokes) randomly on both sides of the stem with the wide end of the nozzle touching the stem.

5. Use red buttercream in a piping bag with a small hole at the tip to pipe the flower centres.

6. Using dark yellow buttercream, pipe short spikes in the centre of each of the flowers.

Tulip

Cultivated in a variety of vibrant colours, shapes and sizes, the tulip is one of the most favoured flowers of all time. The blooms can be single, double, star-like, fringed, elongated and even scented.

To create this flower...

- Colours: for the petals, yellow (Sugarflair Melon); for the leaves, green (Sugarflair Gooseberry)
- Wilton Petal Nozzle 104 and Wilton Leaf Nozzle 352
- Piping bags

1. With the petal nozzle flat on the surface, pipe a yellow pulled petal (see Basic Petal Strokes) of about 2cm (¾in), or longer if you prefer. Pull the nozzle up and away at the tip to curl it.

2. Repeat the same process and pipe a total of three pulled petals for the back of the tulip.

3. For the top petals, repeat the same process again but start by piping the middle one.

4. Then pipe the right and left petals using same technique.

5. Pipe the calyx using the Wilton Leaf Nozzle 352 and green buttercream, pulling slightly back at the tip to give the curled look, as before.

6. Use a cocktail stick to curl the petals if needed be. Do this when the buttercream has crusted.

Primrose

This popular spring flower brings stunning colour to show that winter is over. The colour range and variety is immense, and the flowers are often centred with a contrasting 'eye' or have bands of colours in the petals.

To create this flower...

- Colours: for the petals, yellow (Sugarflair Melon), for the centre, green (Sugarflair Gooseberry) and dark yellow (Sugarflair Melon plus Autumn Leaf)
- Wilton Petal Nozzle 104
- Piping bags

1. Using the nozzle and holding the piping bag at a 20 to 30 degree angle, pipe a heart-shaped petal (see Basic Petal Strokes).

2. Repeat the same process and pipe a total of four heart-shaped petals.

3. Using green buttercream in a piping bag with a small hole at the tip, pipe short spikes in the centre.

4. Use dark yellow buttercream to pipe short lines perpendicular to the tip of the green spikes.

5. Repeat the same process and pipe a few more flowers.

Craspedia

Also called billy buttons or drumstick flowers, the blooms of the craspedia are striking, vibrant hemispheres or even complete globes of tiny flowers. They possess a certain exotic character and add texture to any arrangement.

To create this flower...

- Colours: for the petals, dark yellow (Sugarflair Melon plus Autumn Leaf)
- Writing nozzle 2 (optional)
- Piping bags

1. Pipe a medium-sized mound.

2. Using dark yellow buttercream in a piping bag with a small hole at the tip (or with a writing nozzle), pipe dots around the mound starting from the bottom.

3. Repeat the same process until the whole mound is covered with dots.

4. Repeat the same process and pipe as many flowers as you wish. You may add stems and leaves (see Leaves).

TIP

It is best to pipe the stems first so you know the position of the flower, then add leaves. Make sure to pipe a small blob of buttercream underneath the flower to give it height.

Buttercup

The shiny, waxy textured petals of the buttercup are a bright and vibrant yellow. The apparently complex green and yellow centres can be recreated quite simply, making these cheerful flowers perfect accents for any buttercream design.

To create this flower...

- Colours: for the petals, yellow (Sugarflair Melon); for the centre, green (Sugarflair Gooseberry); for the spikes, dark yellow (Sugarflair Melon plus Autumn Leaf)
- Wilton Petal Nozzle 104
- Piping bags

1. Using a piping bag filled with yellow buttercream, position the nozzle at a 20 to 30 degree angle.

2. Give the piping bag a firm squeeze and pipe a simple petal (see Basic Petal Strokes).

3. Repeat the same process and pipe a total of five petals, starting each one with the wide end of nozzle in the same position as it was for the previous petal.

4. Pipe a small mound of green buttercream in the centre, using a piping bag with a hole at the tip, then pipe small dots over it.

5. Pipe short spikes around the centre, using dark yellow buttercream.

6. Repeat the same process and pipe several flowers close to each other. You can pipe a blob of buttercream underneath subsequent flowers to help with positioning, if necessary.

Snapdragon

These blooms bear a whorl of flowers atop slender stalks and the petals are commonly ruffled on the edges and have a soft texture. You will find them in different heights, from dwarf to tall, and in a wide range of colours.

To create this flower...

- Colours: for the petals, yellow (Sugarflair Melon); for the centre, orange (Sugarflair Orange); for the stem, dark green (Sugarflair Spruce Green)
- PME Petal Nozzle 57R
- Piping bags

1. Using a bag with a small hole at the tip, pipe a stem in dark green. Start at the tip and pipe small buds using enough pressure to make them short and plump, and connect them to the stem.

2. Using the nozzle and yellow buttercream, pipe simple petals (see Basic Petal Strokes) randomly on both sides of the stem with the wide end of the nozzle touching it.

3. To create the flowers at the base, position the first petal on one side of the stem and pipe two or three fan-shaped petals (see Basic Petal Strokes). Repeat to pipe three or four flowers.

4. Repeat the same process making sure that the flowers decrease in number as you progress up the stem and that they are tightly packed without gaps, and overlap.

5. Use orange buttercream in a piping bag with a small hole at the tip to pipe short spikes in the centre of each flower.

Asiatic Lily

These lovely lilies are valued for their flawless, brilliantly coloured flowers. The six petals are either plain or strikingly marked and are often trumpet-shaped, sitting atop tall, erect stems.

To create this flower...

- Colours: for the petals, yellow (Sugarflair Melon); for the centre, dark yellow (Sugarflair Melon plus Autumn Leaf) and green (Sugarflair Gooseberry plus Dark Brown); for the spots, maroon (Sugarflair Brown plus Red)
- Wilton Petal Nozzle 104
- Piping bags

1. Pipe guide marks to help position the six petals.

2. Using yellow buttercream and the nozzle, held at a 20 to 30 degree angle, pipe a rounded two-stroke petal (see Basic Petal Strokes), following your marks.

3. Repeat the same process to pipe the remaining five petals.

4. Using green buttercream in a piping bag with a small hole at the tip, pipe a round flat circle in the centre.

5. Using your maroon buttercream in a piping bag with a small hole at the tip, pipe small dots randomly over each of the petals, except at the outer edges.

6. Pipe short spikes with dark yellow buttercream and use brown buttercream to pipe short lines perpendicular to the tip of the dark yellow spikes.

Black-eyed Susan

Originally a wildflower, this daisy-like plant is now widely cultivated in the garden. The bright yellow petals surround dark brown, almost purplish, central disks of florets – the 'black eye'.

To create this flower...

- Colours: for the petals, yellow (Sugarflair Melon); for the centre brown (Sugarflair Dark Brown) and black (Sugarflair Black)
- PME Leaf Nozzle ST50
- Piping bags

1. To create flowers that are back to back with each other, pipe two blobs of buttercream and two guide circles to help with positioning.

2. Hold your nozzle with the tip touching the first guide circle, give the piping bag a firm squeeze and pipe a leaf technique petal (see Basic Petal Strokes) in yellow.

3. Repeat the same process and pipe petals all around the first guide circle.

4. Pipe a small mound in the centre of the first guide circle using brown buttercream in a piping bag with a small hole cut at the tip.

5. Using black buttercream, pipe a layer of short lines around the brown mound then continue to pipe more layers until the whole mound is covered.

6. Repeat the same process for the second flower.

Hellebore

Sometimes called 'Christmas rose' or 'Lenten rose', the hellebore is a very elegant flower with five showy petal-like sepals surrounded by leafy bracts. Some have flowers with a red-brown edge, others are pastel shades, purples or green.

To create this flower...

- Colours: for the petals, light green (Sugarflair Gooseberry plus Pastel Kiwi) and dark pink (Sugarflair Claret) for a two-tone effect; for the centre, yellow (Sugarflair Melon), green (Sugarflair Gooseberry) and dark yellow (Sugarflair Melon plus Autumn Leaf)
- Wilton Petal Nozzle 126
- Piping bags

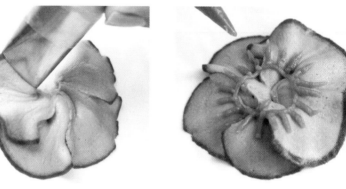

1. Fill a piping bag with the light green and dark pink buttercream (see Two-tone Effect), then holding the nozzle at a 20 to 30 degree angle, pipe a fan-shaped petal (see Basic Petal Strokes).

2. Repeat the same process and pipe five or six subsequent petals that each slightly overlap the previous one.

3. Pipe a guide circle in the centre with about 20 short lines radiating from it, using green buttercream in a piping bag with a small hole at the tip.

4. Pipe very short lines perpendicular to the green lines, using yellow buttercream in a piping bag with a small hole cut at the tip.

5. Pipe one ring of green spikes around the inside of the guide circle. Then use yellow buttercream to pipe the rest of the spikes until the centre is covered.

6. Using dark yellow buttercream, pipe random short spikes in the centre.

Cymbidium Orchid

Orchids are exquisite, but the Cymbidium orchid is one of the most popular because of its delightful blooms. Cymbidium flowers are thick and waxy with five petals on each bloom, and the centre is usually a contrasting colour.

To create this flower...

- Colours: for the petals, green (Sugarflair Gooseberry plus Bittermelon); for the 'lip', untinted buttercream and red (Sugarflair Red) for a two-tone effect; for the 'cap', light green (a hint of Sugarflair Gooseberry); for the centre, red (Sugarflair Red) and yellow (Sugarflair Melon)
- Wilton Petal Nozzles 104 and 126
- Piping bags

1. Pipe a Y-shaped guide mark to help position your first three petals.

2. Using the smaller 126 nozzle held at a 20 to 30 degree angle, pipe a short rounded two-stroke petal (see Basic Petal Strokes) in green, following your marks.

3. Pipe two more petals in two of the gaps between the first petals using the same strokes.

4. In the last gap, using a piping bag filled with the untinted and red buttercream (see Blended Two-tone Effect) and the Wilton 104 Nozzle, pipe a ruffled two-stroke petal (see Basic Petal Strokes) for the 'lip', starting from the centre.

5. Using light green buttercream with the Wilton 104 Nozzle, pipe a small fan-shaped petal (see Basic Petal Strokes) for the 'cap', with the wide end of the nozzle touching the point where the two-tone lip petal ended.

6. Use dark red buttercream in a piping bag with a small hole at the tip to stain the centre and pipe small random dots. Then use yellow buttercream to pipe the two pollination features in the centre.

Cactus

Cacti are evergreen succulents that can blossom with some of the most breathtaking creations. This particular cactus is spherical, heavily ribbed, bluish-green with spines and topped with a yellow flower.

To create this flower...

- Colours: for the plant, dark green (Sugarflair Spruce Green); for the spines, yellow (Sugarflair Melon) or untinted buttercream; for the petals, yellow (Sugarflair Melon); for the flower centre, green (Sugarflair Gooseberry)
- Wilton Leaf Nozzle 352 and Petal Nozzle 103
- Piping bags

1. Pipe a big mound of buttercream or use a ball of cake for the base of the cactus. Then, using dark green buttercream, position the Wilton 352 Nozzle with the two pointed tips against the mound.

2. Continuously squeeze the piping bag as you pull up towards the centre.

3. Repeat the same process until the whole mound is covered, making sure that there are no gaps.

4. Use scissors to trim the top of the mound and create a flat surface.

5. Use yellow or untinted buttercream in a piping bag with a small hole at the tip, and pipe short spikes on the sides of the cactus for the spines.

6. Pipe five simple petals (see Basic Petal Strokes) in yellow, using the Wilton 103 Nozzle, to create a flower on top of the cactus, and add a green centre using a piping bag with a small hole at the tip.

Bells of Ireland

A pretty name for a beautiful plant that is a striking green-yellow. The bells that cling closely to the stems are arranged in whorls of six and the flowers, which are tiny and white, are hidden deep within.

To create this flower...

- Colours: for the petals, green (Sugarflair Gooseberry); for the centre, very light green (a hint of Sugarflair Gooseberry)
- PME Petal Nozzle 58R
- Piping bags

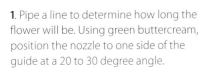

1. Pipe a line to determine how long the flower will be. Using green buttercream, position the nozzle to one side of the guide at a 20 to 30 degree angle.

2. Starting at the base of the stem, pipe a short fan-shaped petal (see Basic Petal Strokes) for the back of the bell and then pipe another on top to create a flower.

3. Repeat the same process and pipe all the flowers on one side of the stem.

4. Pipe all the flowers on the other side, leaving a small gap up the centre.

5. Repeat the same process and pipe the flowers up the centre to cover the gap.

6. Use very light green buttercream in a piping bag with a small hole at the tip, to pipe the spikes in the centre of each of the flowers.

Rock Correa

The tubular bell-shaped flowers of rock correa occur singly or in pairs at the end of short lateral branches. Pale green in colour, this flowering shrub is often used as a low hedge.

To create this flower...

- Colours: for the petals and centre spikes, pale green (Sugarflair Gooseberry); for the tips of the centre spikes, dark yellow (Sugarflair Melon plus Autumn Leaf)
- PME Petal Nozzle 58R
- Piping bags

1. With the nozzle and pale green buttercream, pipe two pulled petals (see Basic Petal Strokes) about 2.5cm (1in) long, next to each other with no gap.

2. Using the same coloured buttercream, but this time in a piping bag with a small hole at the tip, pipe few short lines near the tips of the petals.

3. Using dark yellow buttercream, pipe even shorter lines that are perpendicular to the tip of the light green lines.

4. Pipe another pulled petal on top of the bottom petals, starting at one side. Towards the tip of the petal pull the piping bag outwards to give a slightly curved look.

5. Repeat the same process and pipe the middle petal.

6. Pipe the last petal on the other side using the same process.

Succulents

This is a diverse group of plants, united by their ability to survive in arid conditions. Beyond this, each succulent radiates a certain character that is very distinct. Often it is their extraordinary structure that holds the secret to their charm.

To create this flower...

- Colours: for the petals, green (Sugarflair Gooseberry plus Spruce Green) and brown (Sugarflair Caramel) for a two-tone effect
- Wilton Leaf Nozzle 352
- Piping bag

1. Fill a piping bag with green and brown buttercream (see Two-tone Effect) and determine which way round to hold your nozzle to get the desired dominant colours, or you can alternate them.

2. Pipe a circle as a guide, then position the nozzle at a 20 to 30 degree angle and, with one of the points touching your guide circle, pipe leaf technique petals (see Basic Petal Strokes) to form one layer.

3. Pipe another layer of petals at a slightly steeper angle than the first (30 to 40 degrees), ensuring that they are close to the first layer to avoid any gaps.

TIP
Ideally, you should pipe the petals of the second layer in between the petals in the first layer.

4. Repeat the same process and pipe a few more layers until the centre is covered.

Echeveria

This particular Echeveria is known as 'Blue Rose' and is one of the most attractive succulents, highly valued for its stunning rose-like structure. It normally has tight attractive rosettes of green-grey leaves, which may be edged with red.

To create this flower...

- Colours: for the petals, green (Sugarflair Gooseberry) and red (Sugarflair Claret) for a two-tone effect
- Wilton Nozzle 150
- Flower nail (optional)
- Piping bag

1. Pipe a mound onto a cupcake or flower nail, then with green and red buttercream (see Two-tone Effect), holding the nozzle vertically, and slightly tilted inwards, red stripe uppermost, squeeze while turning the nail counter-clockwise to create a bud.

2. With the nozzle slightly tilted inwards and while turning the flower, pipe an upright curved petal (see Basic Petal Strokes) around the bud. Each petal should overlap the previous one. Pipe two to four short petals.

3. Continue to build up the petals, increasing their size and length as the flower becomes bigger.

4. If it is becoming difficult to pipe in the same direction, you can pipe the petals in a clockwise direction.

5. Repeat the same process and pipe more petals until the flower is as large as you want it to be.

TIP
Make sure that as you pipe the petals around the bud, you also slightly push each petal against the bud so there are no gaps and the flower will not collapse.

Ornamental Cabbage

Large showy plants, ornamental cabbages can be huge! They feature attractive smooth-edged leaves unlike their frilly cousins, ornamental kale, and generally the outer leaves are darker than the centre.

To create this flower...

- Colours: for the first layer of leaves, light pink (Sugarflair Baby Pink); for the second layer, light green (Sugarflair Gooseberry); for the third layer, dark green (Sugarflair Spruce Green)
- Wilton Nozzle 104
- Flower nail (optional)
- Piping bags

1. Pipe a mound of buttercream in the centre of your cupcake (if piping directly onto it) or in the centre of a flower nail.

2. Using light pink buttercream, hold the nozzle vertically with the narrow end up, slightly tilted inwards. Squeeze the piping bag and turn the flower nail or cupcake counter-clockwise to create a bud.

3. With the nozzle vertical, pipe a short, wavy upright petal (see Basic Petal Strokes) around the bud. Each leaf should begin slightly past the middle of the previous one. Pipe two to four short leaves.

4. Change to light green buttercream and repeat the process, piping longer leaves.

5. Swap to dark green buttercream and repeat the same process until you get your desired size of cabbage. Make the leaves even longer as you get further from the centre.

6. If it is becoming difficult to pipe in the same direction, you can pipe the leaves in a clockwise direction.

'Mini Pom' Chrysanthemum

'Yoko Ono' is one of the most popular mini 'pom pom-style' chrysanthemums. These are very cute little flowers and are comprised of brilliant green mini ray petals.

To create this flower...

- Colours: for first layer of petals, bright green (Sugarflair Gooseberry plus Bittermelon); for the second layer, dark green (Sugarflair Spruce Green)
- No nozzle required
- Piping bags

1. Pipe a guide circle with a mound of buttercream in its centre. Using bright green buttercream in a piping bag with a medium-sized hole at the tip, pipe spikes about 0.5cm (¼in) long radiating outwards from the guide circle.

2. Repeat the same process and pipe more layers of spikes in the same colour, but decreasing in length, as you move towards the top of the mound.

3. Change to the dark green buttercream when you near the top and continue the same process, angling the spikes towards the centre.

4. Pipe the stem in dark green.

TIP
If you want to include leaves and stems, these should be piped first. You don't need a nozzle to create this flower, but if you want to use one, choose a writing nozzle, size 1, 2 or 3.

Spurge

Leafy spurge flowers are small, yellowish-green and arranged in numerous tiny clusters. They are surrounded by pairs of yellow green, heart-shaped bracts that are often mistaken for the plant's flowers.

To create this flower...

- Colours: for the petals and centre, bright green (Sugarflair Gooseberry plus Bittermelon); for the centre spikes, light green (Sugarflair Spruce Green); for the flowers, yellow (Sugarflair Melon)
- PME Petal Nozzles 57R and 58R and PME Nozzle 42
- Piping bags

1. Using the smaller PME 58R Nozzle and bright green buttercream, hold the piping bag at a 20 to 30 degree angle and pipe a short curved petal (see Basic Petal Strokes).

2. Repeat to pipe another petal opposite the first with a small gap in the middle.

3. Using the larger PME 57R Nozzle, pipe a short fan-shaped petal (see Basic Petal Strokes) on top of one of the short curved petals in bright green buttercream.

4. Repeat the same process and pipe the same short fan-shaped petal on the other short curved petal, making sure that you cover the gap in the middle.

5. Pipe two centre spikes in the middle, using light green buttercream in a piping bag with a small hole at the tip.

6. Use yellow buttercream with the PME 42 Nozzle to pipe two small simple stars for flowers.

Cornflower

The attractive blooms of the cornflower are an eye-catching bright blue. The star-like flowers feature outer bracts that are fringed and have a dark margin.

To create this flower...

- Colours: for the petals and spikes, blue (Sugarflair Deep Purple); for the centre, dark blue (Sugarflair Navy Blue) and purple (Sugarflair Deep Purple plus Violet)
- PME Petal Nozzle 57R
- Piping bags

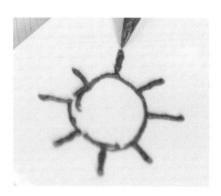

1. Pipe a guide circle with about eight short, evenly spaced lines radiating from it. The radiating lines should be about 0.5cm (¼in) long.

2. Hold the piping bag at a 20 to 30 degree angle, with the wide end of the nozzle touching one of the lines a little outside the circle. Pipe three to five short pulled petals (see Basic Petal Strokes) in blue.

3. Fill the centre by piping a small mound of buttercream using dark blue.

4. Starting from the outer edge of the central mound and working inwards, pipe short spikes using dark blue buttercream in a bag with a small hole at the tip.

5. Using purple buttercream in a bag with a small hole at the tip, overpipe the short lines from the edge of the central mound to the base of the petals, and add a few more spikes to the centre.

6. Use a cocktail stick (toothpick) to smooth the edges of each petal after the buttercream has crusted.

Delphinium

Grown for their showy spikes of colourful summer flowers in gorgeous shades of blue, pink, white and purple, delphiniums may produce single or double flowers, and some blossoms sport dramatic black or white centres.

To create this flower...

- Colours: for the petals, dark blue (Sugarflair Deep Purple plus Baby Blue); for the centres, untinted buttercream
- PME Petal Nozzle 58R
- Piping bags

1. Pipe a guide line to determine how long you want the flower to be. Using dark blue buttercream in your piping bag, position the nozzle to one side of the guide and hold it at a 20 to 30 degree angle.

2. Pipe a short fan-shaped petal (see Basic Petal Strokes) for the bottom and then another on top of it to create a flower.

3. Repeat the same process to pipe all the flowers on one side of the guide line.

4. Continue to pipe all the flowers on the other side, leaving a small gap up the centre.

5. Fill the gap with an upright wavy petal (see Basic Petal Strokes) to give the middle of the flower some body, then pipe flowers up the centre to cover the gap.

6. Use untinted buttercream in a bag with a small hole at the tip to pipe the very short spikes in the centre of each flower.

Iris

Beautiful Irises produce dramatic and brilliant blooms, with a characteristic exotic fan-shape consisting of one or more symmetrical six-lobed flowers. They come in a wide variety of colours but the best-known ones are blue, purple and yellow.

To create this flower...

- Colours: for the petals, blue (Sugarflair Baby Blue plus Navy Blue) and yellow (Sugarflair Melon plus Autumn Leaf); for the spots, dark blue (Sugarflair Navy Blue)
- Wilton Petal Nozzle 104
- Piping bags

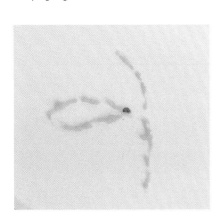

1. Pipe a guide mark to help with the positioning of the two side petals and the middle petal.

2. Using the Wilton 104 Nozzle and blue buttercream, pipe a rounded two-stroke petal (see Basic Petal Strokes) for the middle petal.

3. Pipe elongated two-stroke petals on either side of the middle petal.

4. Pipe two or three wavy upright petals (see Basic Petal Strokes), about 2–2.5cm (¾–1in) long, that touch the base of the middle petal. Then pipe a short upright petal at the base of the other two petals. They can slightly overlap.

5. Use yellow buttercream in a piping bag with a small hole at the tip to pipe the yellow patch in the middle of each of the big two-stroke petals.

6. Using dark blue buttercream in a bag with a small hole at the tip, pipe small dots on the sides of the outer upright petals to complete the flower.

Blue Star

These blooms are one of the truest blues you will find in the garden. The flowers of blue star, or amsonia, are clusters of small, star-shaped blossoms, borne on top of tall stems, which make perfect eye-catching centrepieces.

To create this flower...

- Colours: for the petals, blue (Sugarflair Deep Purple); for the centre, yellow (Sugarflair Melon); for the stems, green (Sugarflair Gooseberry)
- PME Petal Nozzle 57R
- Piping bags

1. Fill a piping bag with blue buttercream and hold the nozzle at a 20 degree angle with the wide end down.

2. Pipe five or six short pulled petals (see Basic Petal Strokes) that join together with a common centre.

3. Repeat the same process to pipe more flowers. To give them volume, pipe a small blob of buttercream underneath or pipe some flowers on top of the each other.

4. Using yellow buttercream in a piping bag with a small hole at the tip, pipe a small dot in the centre of each flower.

5. Pipe a stem or stems using green buttercream in a piping bag with a small hole at the tip.

6. Use a cocktail stick (toothpick) to smooth the edges of each petal when the buttercream has crusted.

Hydrangea

Mophead or lace-cap, hydrangeas possess a charm which we all find completely irresistible. Shades of blue, pink, white and purple can sometimes be found on a single shrub. The actual flower is really small but is surrounded by colourful bracts.

To create this flower...

- Colours: for the petals, light blue (Sugarflair Baby Blue) and pale green (Sugarflair Gooseberry) for a two-tone effect; for the centre, blue (Sugarflair Baby Blue)
- PME Petal Nozzle 103
- Piping bags

1. Fill a piping bag with light blue and untinted buttercream (see Two-tone Effect) and, using the nozzle held at a 20 to 30 degree angle, pipe a small fan-shape petal (see Basic Petal Strokes).

2. Repeat the same process and pipe three or four more petals that all start from the same point.

3. Repeat to pipe more flowers that are close together and sometimes overlap to create the characteristic hydrangea pom-pom bloom.

4. Using blue buttercream in a piping bag with a small hole at the tip, pipe small dots in the centre of each flower.

TIP
In reality, Hydrangeas have large leaves that you would need to pipe first before piping the flowers, but you may also pipe small leaves in between the gaps of the flowers to give the impression of foliage.

Brunnera

The very delicate looking flowers of brunnera have five petals, which come in a range of blues from pastel to dark and vibrant. Each has a white centre, giving them an appearance not unlike Forget-me-nots.

To create this flower...

- Colours: for the petals, blue (Sugarflair Deep Purple); for the centres, black (Sugarflair Black) and untinted buttercream; for the stems, green (Sugarflair Gooseberry)
- PME Petal Nozzle 57R
- Piping bags

1. Pipe the stems using green buttercream in a bag with a small hole at the tip.

2. Using the nozzle and blue buttercream, hold the piping bag at a 20 degree angle and pipe five simple petals (see Basic Petal Strokes) that join together with a common centre.

3. Repeat the same process to pipe more flowers. To give volume, pipe a small blob of buttercream and pipe a flower on top, or overlap some of them.

4. Using plain buttercream in a piping bag with a small hole at the tip, pipe a small dot in the centre of each flower.

5. Pipe an even smaller dot of black in each of the white centres.

Buddleia

The flowers of the butterfly bush, as buddleia is also known, are magnets for butterflies and hummingbirds. The drooping flower-spikes are honey-scented and come in shades of blue, pink, white, red and include some very attractive bi-coloured blooms.

To create this flower...

- Colours: for the petals, blue (Sugarflair Baby Blue plus Navy Blue); for the centres, orange (Sugarflair Orange)
- PME Petal Nozzle 57R
- Piping bags

1. Pipe a curved guide line to determine how long you want the flower-spike to be. Fill a piping bag with blue buttercream and position the nozzle to one side of the guide at a 20 to 30 degree angle.

2. Pipe a short fan-shaped petal (see Basic Petal Strokes) to make the bottom and then another on top of it to create a flower.

3. Repeat the process to pipe all the flowers on one side of the guide line.

4. Repeat to pipe all the flowers on the other side, leaving a small gap up the centre of the flower-spike.

5. Fill the gap with an upright wavy petal (see Basic Petal Strokes) to give volume in the centre of the flower-spike. Then pipe flowers, as before, up the centre to cover the upright wavy petal.

6. Use orange buttercream in a bag with a small hole at the tip to pipe the very short spikes in the centre of each flower.

Bluebell

With their tubular shape and sweet scent, bluebells are a spectacle of nature. Almost all of the flower heads appear on one side of the stem, making it bend over.

To create this flower...

- Colours: for the stem and calyx, light green (Sugarflair Gooseberry); for the petals, blue-violet (Sugarflair Deep Purple, plus a of hint of Baby Blue)
- PME Petal Nozzle 57R
- Piping bags

1. Snip the end off a piping bag, so that you are left with a fine tip. Using light green buttercream, pipe the stems.

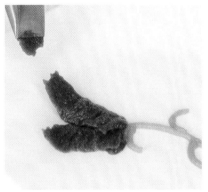

2. Using the blue-purple buttercream and nozzle, pipe two short, pulled petals (see Basic Petal Strokes) in the same direction. Pull the piping bag back to create a curled effect on the ends.

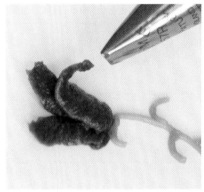

3. Repeat step 2, but this time pipe two petals of the same length on top of the first ones.

4. Repeat steps 2 and 3 and pipe a few more flowers, facing the same direction.

5. Using the same bag and light green buttercream used in step 1, pipe the calyx for each flower.

Morning Glory

As the name suggests, the fragrant, trumpet-like flowers of morning glory are at their best in the earlier part of the day, unfurling like little umbrellas in the morning and often lasting little more than 24 hours.

To create this flower...

- Colours: for the petals, blue (Sugarflair Deep Purple plus Baby Blue) and untinted buttercream for a two-tone effect; for the centre, yellow (Sugarflair Melon plus Autumn Leaf) and untinted buttercream
- Wilton Petal Nozzle 126
- Piping bags

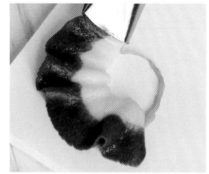

1. Pipe a guide circle to determine how big your flower will be.

2. Fill a piping bag with blue and untinted buttercream (see Two-tone Effect) and holding the nozzle at a 20 to 30 degree angle with the wide end touching the guide, pipe a long curved petal (see Basic Petal Strokes) all around the guide circle.

3. Continue piping around the guide circle until both ends meet (see tip below), then pull the nozzle inwards toward the centre so the join is not obvious.

TIP
When piping the long curved petal in steps 2 and 3, you can stop and start again whenever you need to – it doesn't need to be a continuous circle.

4. Use yellow buttercream in a piping bag with a small hole at the tip to pipe the yellow patch in the centre of the flower.

5. Pipe three short spikes in the centre of the flower using untinted buttercream in a bag with a medium hole at the tip.

Forget-me-not

The flowers of forget-me-nots are usually small, blue, five petalled and have yellow centres. The plant has a habit of appearing in a slightly unruly fashion where you least expect it, but the cheerful clusters of flowers are always attractive.

To create this flower...

- Colours: for the petals, light blue (Sugarflair Baby Blue); for the centres, yellow (Sugarflair Melon), black (Sugarflair Black) and untinted buttercream
- Wilton Petal Nozzle 103
- Piping bags

1. Fill a piping bag with light blue buttercream and hold the nozzle at a 20 to 30 degree angle.

2. Give the bag a firm squeeze and pipe a simple petal (see Basic Petal Strokes).

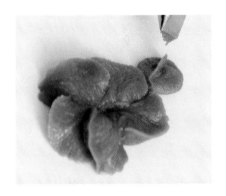

3. Repeat the same process and pipe a total of five petals from a common central point, always starting with the wide end of the nozzle at the same angle as it was for your first petal.

4. Repeat the same process and pipe several flowers close to each other. You can pipe a blob of buttercream to give extra height and pipe a flower on top.

5. Using untinted buttercream in a piping bag with a small hole at the tip, pipe about five short lines in between the petals which all radiate from the centre.

6. Pipe a small circle in the centre of each of the flowers with yellow buttercream, then pipe a smaller black dot in the centre of each yellow circle.

Scabious

Also known as the pincushion flower, the blooms of Scabiosa, commonly called scabious, really do resemble the rounded shape of a cushion with pin-like stamens. These are stunning flowers that stand out in any arrangement.

To create this flower...

- Colours: for the petals, blue-violet (Sugarflair Deep Purple); for the centre and spikes, pale brown (Sugarflair Caramel)
- Wilton Petal Nozzle 104
- Piping bags

1. Pipe a guide circle, then with blue-violet buttercream in your piping bag, position the nozzle at a 20 to 30 degree angle with the wide end touching the circle.

2. Pipe a row of ruffle petals (see Basic Petal Strokes) following the guide circle.

3. Repeat the same process and pipe two or three more layers of petals at an increasingly acute angle, each one close to the previous layer.

4. Use a cocktail stick (toothpick) and touch the edges of the petals randomly to give a more natural rough-edged look.

5. Pipe a mound of pale brown buttercream in the centre of the flower.

6. Using a piping bag with a small hole at the tip, pipe small dots in pale brown to cover the mound and short spikes around the edge of the centre.

Lisianthus

Also known as Texas bluebell or prairie gentian, lisianthus is a long-stemmed flower, popular in floral arrangements and a native of the warm southern states of the USA. The flowers are large and bell-shaped with flaring petals and yellow centres.

To create this flower...

- Colours: for the petals, deep violet (Sugarflair Deep Purple plus Grape Violet) and untinted buttercream for a two-tone effect; for the centre, green (Sugarflair Gooseberry) and yellow (Sugarflair Melon plus Autumn Leaf)
- Wilton Petal Nozzle 104
- Piping bags

1. Pipe a guide circle, then with deep violet and untinted buttercream in your piping bag (see Blended Two-tone Effect), position the nozzle at a 20 to 30 degree angle with the wide end touching the circle.

2. Pipe a layer of slightly wavy curved petals (see Basic Petal Strokes) following the guide circle.

3. Repeat the same process and pipe a few more layers, alternating slightly wavy and straight curved petals.

4. Pipe short, fat spikes in the centre using green buttercream in a bag with a small hole at the tip.

5. Pipe a few yellow spikes in between the green ones.

Clematis

This popular garden climber has a fragrant smell and unique appearance, with large blue-purple flowers of between five and nine petals.

To create this flower...

- Colours: for the petals, blue-purple (Sugarflair Deep Purple plus a hint of Baby Blue); for the stigma, caramel (Sugarflair Caramel plus a hint of Gooseberry); for the long stamens, violet (Sugarflair Grape Violet); for the stem and short stamens, light green (Sugarflair Gooseberry)
- Wilton Leaf Nozzle 352
- Piping bags

1. Pipe a circle as a guide for the size of your flower. Position the nozzle at a 45 degree angle and pipe a medium-sized blue-purple petal.

2. Pipe more petals close to each other completely covering the guide circle. The number of petals will depend on the size of your circle.

3. Using the caramel buttercream, pipe a small mound in the centre of the flower, leaving a gap between it and the petals.

4. Pipe stamens using violet in a piping bag with a small hole at the tip. Start from the edge of the mound and finish halfway up the petals. Pipe two layers.

5. Use light green buttercream to pipe short stamens in the opposite direction, ending in the centre of the mound. Repeat all the way around.

6. Pipe short green stamens, starting from the same central point as in step 4, but stopping halfway along the purple stamens. If required, pipe another layer.

Columbine

Found in many shades, including some delightful bi-coloured examples, columbines are also known as granny's bonnets. They make a lovely addition to a cottage garden with their classic and intricate appearance.

To create this flower...

- Colours: for the petals, deep violet (Sugarflair Deep Purple) and white (Sugarflair Super White); for the centre, yellow (Sugarflair Melon)
- Wilton Petal Nozzle 104
- Piping bags

1. Pipe a guide circle and radiating guide marks for five evenly spaced petals.

2. Using deep violet, hold the nozzle at a 20 to 30 degree angle, with the wide end touching your guide circle, and pipe a two-stroke petal (see Basic Petal Strokes) about 2.5–3cm (1–1¼in) long.

3. Repeat the same process and pipe a total of five petals of the same length.

4. Using white buttercream, and with the wide end of the nozzle pointing outwards, pipe five short curved petals (see Basic Petal Strokes) in between the long petals leaving a small gap in the centre.

5. Pipe short spikes in the centre of the flower using yellow buttercream and a piping bag with a small hole at the tip.

Phlox

Typically five-petalled, the phlox comes in many colours and shapes – some plants are quite tall while others are creeping in habit. The masses of bright star-shaped flowers add dimension and volume to any arrangement.

To create this flower...

- Colours: for the petals, blue-violet (Sugarflair Deep Purple plus Baby Blue); for the centres, dark blue (Sugarflair Navy Blue) and yellow (Sugarflair Melon plus Autumn Leaf); for the stems, green (Sugarflair Gooseberry)
- PME Petal Nozzle 58R
- Piping bags

1. Using green buttercream in a piping bag with a small hole at the tip, pipe the stems. Then pipe a couple of simple buds randomly up the sides of the stems using blue-violet buttercream.

2. Create your first flower by piping five simple petals (see Basic Petal Strokes) that join at one central point, using blue-violet buttercream and the nozzle.

3. Repeat the same process and pipe a few more flowers to create a good cluster.

4. Using dark blue buttercream in a piping bag with a small hole at the tip, pipe dots in the centre of each flower. Also, pipe tiny dark blue calyxes on the buds.

5. Pipe even smaller yellow dots on the dark blue dots in the flower centres.

Spiderwort

The flowers of spiderwort have three oval petals and come in a range of colours, all with yellow anthers at the centre. They grow in clusters which gives them impact despite the small size of the individual flowers.

To create this flower...

- Colours: for the petals, blue-violet (Sugarflair Grape Violet plus Navy Blue); for the centres, dark violet (Sugarflair Grape Violet) and yellow (Sugarflair Melon plus Autumn Leaf)
- Wilton Petal Nozzle 104
- Piping bags

1. Pipe guide marks in a Y-shape to help with the positioning the three petals.

2. Hold the piping bag at a 20 to 30 degree angle, with the nozzle in a 10 o'clock position, and pipe a non-ruffled two-stroke petal (see Basic Petal Strokes).

3. Repeat to pipe a total of three petals of equal length, leaving no gaps in between.

4. Use dark violet buttercream in a piping bag with a small hole at the tip to pipe short spikes in the centre.

5. Pipe a small dot at the tip of each spike using yellow buttercream.

Nightshade Flower

The deep violet or bluish-purple flowers of nightshade have five petals and yellow centres. The structure of the flower is unusual as, after slowly opening, the petals eventually curl right back to almost touch the stem.

To create this flower...

- Colours: for the petals, deep violet (Sugarflair Deep Purple); for the centres, green (Sugarflair Gooseberry), dark blue (Sugarflair Navy), and yellow (Sugarflair Melon and Autumn Leaf)
- PME Petal Nozzle 57R
- Piping bags

1. Using deep violet buttercream, hold the nozzle at a 20 degree angle, with the wide end downwards, and pipe a short pulled petal (see Basic Petal Strokes).

2. Pipe a total of five short pulled petals that join together at a common central point.

3. Repeat to pipe more flowers. To give them volume, pipe a small blob of buttercream underneath one or two, or pipe some flowers on top of others.

4. Pipe short lines in the centre of each flower using green buttercream in a piping bag with a small hole at the tip. Using dark blue buttercream, pipe a small circle in each flower centre.

5. Pipe a single thick spike in the centre of each of the flowers using yellow buttercream and firm pressure on the piping bag.

6. Use a cocktail stick (toothpick) to smooth the edges of each petal when the buttercream has crusted.

Violet

The view of a densely planted area of violets is stunning. They come in different colours, but as the name suggests, violet is the most common. The gently drooping flowers have five rounded petals and a yellow centre.

To create this flower...

- Colours: for the petals, violet (Sugarflair Grape Violet); for the centre, yellow (Sugarflair Melon plus Autumn Leaf)
- Wilton Petal Nozzle 104
- Piping bags

1. Using violet buttercream in a piping bag, hold the petal nozzle at a 20 to 30 degree angle.

2. Give the piping bag a firm squeeze and pipe a simple fan-shaped petal (see Basic Petal Strokes).

3. Repeat to pipe a total of five petals, keeping the position of the wide end of the nozzle the same for all the petals.

4. Repeat to pipe several flowers close to each other. You can pipe a blob of buttercream underneath a flower to give depth if necessary, or pipe some flowers on top of others.

5. Using yellow buttercream in a piping bag with small hole at the tip, pipe four or five short spikes at each flower centre.

Pansy

A real favourite in the garden, pansies are popular for their bright colours and happy 'face' created by the dark markings in the centre of some varieties.

To create this flower...

- Colours: for the petals, blue (Sugarflair Baby Blue plus Navy Blue) and yellow, (Sugarflair Melon plus Autumn Leaf); for the centre, blue-purple (Sugarflair Navy Blue) and untinted buttercream
- Wilton Petal Nozzles 103 and 104
- Piping bags

1. Using the Wilton 104 Nozzle and blue-purple buttercream, pipe two simple petals (see Basic Petal Strokes) beside each other.

2. From the base of the first two petals, pipe a short curved petal (see Basic Petal Strokes) using yellow buttercream and the Wilton 104 Nozzle.

3. Change to the Wilton 103 Nozzle and with yellow buttercream pipe two simple petals on top of the blue petals.

4. Repeat the same process and pipe a few more flowers close to each other.

5. Using blue-purple buttercream in a piping bag with a small hole at the tip, pipe short lines radiating from the centre of each flower.

6. In the centre of each of the flowers, pipe two short but thick curved lines facing each other in untinted buttercream in a piping bag with a small hole at the tip.

Primula

Relatives of the common primrose, Primulas come in a variety of different colours, including purple, white and yellow. Many of them are centred with a contrasting yellow eye while others have narrow bands of colour in the petals.

To create this flower...

- Colours: for the petals, violet (Sugarflair Grape Violet plus Baby Blue) and untinted buttercream for a two-tone effect; centre, dark yellow (Sugarflair Melon plus Autumn Leaf) and green (Sugarflair Gooseberry)
- Wilton Petal Nozzle 104
- Piping bags

1. Pipe a guide circle with radiating marks for the five petals. Fill a piping bag with both violet and untinted buttercream (see Two-tone Effect), and hold the piping bag at a 20 to 30 degree angle with the wide end of the nozzle pointing downwards.

2. Pipe a heart-shaped petal (see Basic Petal Strokes).

3. Repeat the same process and pipe a total of five heart-shaped petals following your guide marks.

4. Use dark yellow buttercream in a piping bag with a small hole at the tip to pipe a circle in the centre of the flower.

5. Fill the centre of the circle with green buttercream.

Lavender

Most lavender flowers are purple but sometimes they may be white, blue or even pink. They are borne on slender stems in neat spikes above green-grey foliage. Lavender is most highly prized for its heady fragrance.

To create this flower...

- Colours: for the petals, purple (Sugarflair Grape Violet); for the main stem, green (Sugarflair Gooseberry); for the short stems, dark violet (Sugarflair Grape Violet)
- PME Petal Nozzle 57R
- Piping bags

1. Using green buttercream in a piping bag with a small hole at the tip, pipe the main stems.

2. Using dark violet buttercream, pipe thick lines about 0.5cm (¼in) long, starting from the tip of each stem.

3. Using violet buttercream and the petal nozzle, pipe the flowers at the tip of each dark violet stem. Each flower is created by piping two or three simple petals (see Basic Petal Strokes) on top of each other.

4. Repeat the same process and pipe more flower spikes.

TIP
Because these flowers are piped with a small nozzle, making them fairly light, you can pipe them on the side of the cake. If you do, make sure to pipe them first before any other flower, and remember to apply sufficient pressure as you pipe so that they really stick to the cake.

Aster

Dainty aster flowers are actually a collection of very tiny tubular flowers, grouped together in a central disk, and surrounded by so-called ray petals. They come in a rainbow of colours including purple, white, lavender, red and pink.

To create this flower...

- Colours: for the petals, violet (Sugarflair Grape Violet); for the centre, yellow (Sugarflair Melon plus Autumn Leaf)
- PME Petal Nozzle 57R
- Piping bags

1. Pipe a guide circle, then holding the piping bag and nozzle at a 20 degree angle, pipe a ring of pulled petals (see Basic Petal Strokes) in violet.

2. Repeat the same process and pipe another layer of petals on top of the first.

3. Pipe more flowers, with guide circles to help position the petals. To give volume, pipe a small blob of buttercream underneath, or pipe some flowers on top of each other.

4. Using yellow buttercream in a bag with a small hole at the tip, pipe dots until it creates a small dome in the centre.

5. Use a cocktail stick (toothpick) to smooth the edges of each petal when the buttercream has crusted.

Day Lily

This variety of day lily, 'Purple de Oro', has a very sophisticated flower, the rich purple blooms of which have a dark purple lining and pale purple midribs. The petals usually have white tips, which add to the glamour.

To create this flower...

- Colours: for the outer petals, purple (Sugarflair Grape Violet); for the central petals, purple (Sugarflair Grape Violet) and untinted buttercream for a two-tone effect; for the centre, light green (Sugarflair Gooseberry), brown (Sugarflair Gooseberry and Dark Brown) and purple (Sugarflair Grape Violet)
- Wilton Petal Nozzle 104
- Piping bags

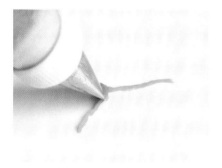

1. Pipe a Y-shaped mark for your first three petals.

2. Hold your nozzle and piping bag at a 20 to 30 degree angle and pipe three rounded two-stroke petals (see Basic Petal Strokes) about 2.5–3cm (1–1¼in) long, following the guide marks.

3. Fill a piping bag with purple and untinted buttercream (see Two-tone Effect) and, in between the first three petals, pipe three ruffled rounded two-stroke petals, starting from the centre.

4. Using light green buttercream in a piping bag with a small hole at the tip, fill the gap in the centre.

5. Use brown buttercream in a piping bag with a small hole at the tip to pipe three to five short but thick lines in the centre, and dark purple buttercream to pipe a short line at the tip of each of the lines.

Fuchsia

The violet petals of the fuchsia contrast dramatically with its crimson sepals, making a magnificent display of colour. Fuchsias have four slender sepals and four broader petals.

To create this flower...

- Colours: for the stamens, claret (Sugarflair Claret) and violet (Sugarflair Grape Violet); for the petals, violet (Sugarflair Grape Violet); for the sepals, claret (Sugarflair Claret)
- Wilton Petal Nozzle 103
- Piping bags

1. Using a piping bag with a small hole at the tip and claret buttercream, pipe short lines to create the stamens.

2. Pipe small dots at the tip of each of the stamens using the violet buttercream.

3. Using the violet buttercream and nozzle, hold the piping bag at a 40 degree angle. Squeeze the bag gently while slowly pulling away and then gently fold back in the middle. Repeat on the other side.

4. Pipe three or four short pulled petals (see Basic Petal Strokes) in claret, starting from the base of the flower. Each stroke should be pulled outwards to make a curl.

5. Using claret buttercream, pipe the tube of the flower. Apply continuous pressure as you slowly pull away the piping bag.

6. When the buttercream has crusted, use a cocktail stick (toothpick) to enhance the curls of the pulled petals you created in step 4.

Allium

Also known as ornamental onions, allium come in purples and blues, pinks, whites and greens. The flowers have a distinctive round shape and are borne on straight stems in a variety of heights and sizes.

To create this flower...

- Colours: for the stems, green (Sugarflair Gooseberry); for the flower, purple (Sugarflair Grape Violet); for the spikes, light purple (Sugarflair Grape Violet)
- PME Nozzle 42
- Piping bags

1. Pipe a guide circle and stems, using green buttercream in a piping bag with a small hole at the tip.

2. Using purple buttercream, hold the piping bag and nozzle at a 90 degree angle and gently squeeze with even pressure to create a star.

3. Repeat the same process and pipe a ring of stars following the guide circle, making sure there are no gaps.

4. Pipe a mound in the centre, using the same nozzle, to give the flower a rounded dome shape.

5. Cover the central mound with piped stars in purple buttercream.

6. Using light purple buttercream in a bag with a small hole at the tip, pipe random short spikes, then overpipe the stems again to make them thicker.

Wisteria

The pendulous clusters of fragrant petals that hang from the wisteria plant are like bunches of grapes. Each wisteria flower is pea-like, and varieties of this enchanting wall-climber come in violet, purple, bluish-purple, pink, blue and white.

To create this flower...

- Colours: for the petals, light purple (Sugarflair Lilac) and dark purple (Sugarflair Grape Violet)
- Wilton Leaf Nozzle 352
- Piping bags

1. Pipe a guide for the size and length of your flower. The shape should be wider at the top and narrow to a pointed tip at the bottom

2. Hold the nozzle at a 90 degree angle with two points touching the surface at the wide end of your guide shape. Squeeze firmly and pipe a small leaf technique petal (see Basic Petal Strokes) in light purple.

3. Pipe more petals that are really tightly packed together to fill the guide shape from the top to about the middle.

4. Swap to the darker purple buttercream and continue to pipe the petals down to the tip end of the guide shape.

5. Add a few random dark purple petals nearer the wider top of the flower, making them more pointed.

Passion Flower

The extraordinarily intricate structure of Passiflora has made them a popular garden climber, and they look really exotic. These flowers have a wide, flat petal base with a complex centre featuring many different coloured elements.

To create this flower...

- Colours: for the petals, pale violet (Sugarflair Grape Violet); for the spikes, purple (Sugarflair Grape Violet), plain buttercream and blue (Sugarflair Navy Blue); for the centre, green (Sugarflair Gooseberry) and dark green (Sugarflair Spruce Green)
- Wilton Petal Nozzle 104
- Piping bags

1. Pipe a guide circle and with the nozzle at 10 to 20 degree angle, pipe a pulled petal (see Basic Petal Strokes) about 2.5–3cm (1–1¼in) long in pale violet.

2. Repeat to pipe petals all around the guide circle. Then fill the centre with dark violet tinted buttercream, using a piping bag with a small hole at the tip.

3. Pipe short lines from the centre radiating out about 1cm (½in).

4. Extend the lines using untinted buttercream, then blue at the tips.

5. Using light green buttercream, pipe a small circle in the middle.

6. Using dark green buttercream, pipe five or six short lines in the centre. Use light green to pipe short lines perpendicular to the tip of the dark green lines.

Limonium

The long-lasting blossoms of limonium can be found in violet, white, pink, yellow and purple. This hardy plant can thrive in saline soils, hence the common names of sea lavender or marsh rosemary.

To create this flower...

- Colours: for the petals, purple (Sugarflair Grape Violet); for the stem and calyx, green (Sugarflair Gooseberry)
- PME Nozzle 5 and Petal Nozzle 58R, and Wilton Petal Nozzle 103
- Piping bags

1. Pipe a stem using the PME Nozzle 5 and green buttercream, to determine how long you want the flower to be.

2. Using purple buttercream, mark the positions for the placement of the flowers, about 1cm (½in) out from the stem.

3. Pipe four to six upright and simple petals with a slight overlap (see Basic Petal Strokes) on each of the marked guides using the Wilton Petal Nozzle 103 and purple buttercream.

4. Repeat the same process and finish all the flowers.

5. Using green buttercream with the PME 58R Nozzle, pipe two or three pulled petals (see Basic Petal Strokes) from the stem to the base of each flower.

Ornamental Kale

Ornamental kale is not technically a flower but we had to include it, as its ruffled rose-like appearance makes it extremely beautiful and popular in modern bridal bouquets.

To create this flower...

- Colours: for most of the petals, lilac (Sugarflair Lilac plus a hint of Grape Violet); for the remaining petals and bud, light green (Sugarflair Gooseberry) and lilac (Sugarflair Grape Violet) for a two-tone effect
- Wilton Petal Nozzle 104
- Flower nail (optional)
- Piping bags

1. Pipe a mound of buttercream onto the centre of a cupcake or flower nail. Fill a piping bag with both lilac and light green buttercream (see Tone-tone Effect).

2. Hold the nozzle vertically with the wide end touching the surface and pipe two upright curved petals (see Basic Petal Strokes) for the bud, making them overlap slightly.

3. Using lilac buttercream, pipe further arch-shaped petals (see Basic Petal Strokes) turning the cupcake or nail and moving up and down for ruffled edges. Pipe two to four short overlapping petals.

4. Continue piping the arched ruffled petals. As the flower becomes bigger, your petals will become longer and the angle of the nozzle will decrease.

5. Use the two-tone light green and lilac buttercream to create the final outer petals, using ruffled petal strokes.

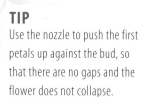

TIP
Use the nozzle to push the first petals up against the bud, so that there are no gaps and the flower does not collapse.

Bougainvillea

The flowers of bougainvillea are tubular and may come in shades of purple, white, red, yellow and pink and even mixed colours. Each is surrounded by three colourful paper-like bracts, which are usually mistaken as the actual flowers.

To create this flower...

- Colours: for the petals, purple (Sugarflair Lilac); for the centre spikes, dark purple (Sugarflair Grape Violet); for the centres, untinted buttercream and yellow, (Sugarflair Melon)
- Wilton Leaf Nozzle 352 and PME 5 Nozzle
- Piping bags

1. Using purple buttercream, hold the piping bag and nozzle at a 20 to 30 degree angle with one of the tips of the nozzle touching the surface.

2. Give the piping bag a firm squeeze and pipe a leaf technique petal (see Basic Petal Strokes).

3. Repeat the same process and pipe a total of three petals to make a flower.

4. Pipe more flowers, making sure they are close to each other and overlap a little.

5. Using dark purple buttercream, pipe three or four short spikes starting from the centre.

6. Using the PME 5 Nozzle and untinted buttercream, pipe two or three stars in the centre of each flower. Pipe a dot on top of each star using yellow in a bag with a small hole at the tip.

LEAVES

Foliage can perform several functions in a design. You can use leaves to really set up or frame a flower, or to fill spaces between design elements. We've given some examples of filler foliage on the opposite page, and show how you can use it in the cake projects at the end of this book. Below you can see which nozzles to choose to create different leaf shapes. See the nozzle chart at the beginning of the book to see what each of the nozzles looks like.

Pine tree

Green Amaranthus

Climbing leaves

Pussy willow

Wheat

Cat tails

Ferns

Contemporary Cake

This dramatic modern cake is a real showstopper. The flowers soften the strong lines but the bold colours make for an impactful design that features the techniques of carving, creating texture and blending buttercream colours, as well as piping flowers. To create this sculpted masterpiece, you need a dense cake, such as Madeira, as a regular sponge will not carve well.

SIMPLE MADEIRA (DENSE) CAKE RECIPE

You will need...

350g (12oz) unsalted butter
250g (12oz) caster (superfine) sugar
250g (12oz) self-raising (-rising) flour
125g (6oz) plain (all-purpose) flour
5 large eggs
⅛ tsp salt
2–3 tbsp milk

Greaseproof (wax) paper
20cm (8in) round cake tin
Mixer (hand-held or stand)
Mixing bowls
Measuring spoons
Skewer (optional)

1. Pre-heat the oven to 160°C/325°F/Gas Mark 3. Grease and line the base of your cake tin with greaseproof (wax) paper, and grease the paper.

2. Sift the flours together with the salt in a mixing bowl. Set aside.

3. In another large mixing bowl, use a mixer to cream the butter and sugar together until light, fluffy and pale. Beat in the eggs, one at a time. Beat the mixture well between each one and adding a tablespoon of the flour with the last egg to prevent the mixture curdling.

4. Combine the wet and dry ingredients by sifting in the flours and salt into a second mixing bowl.

5. Gently fold in, using enough milk to give a mixture that falls slowly from the spoon.

6. Transfer the mixture to the lined cake tin and bake for 60–90 minutes. Check your cake is ready by seeing if it is well risen, firm to the touch and if a skewer inserted into the centre will come out clean.

7. Turn the cake out onto a wire rack and leave to cool completely.

You will need to stack, fill and freeze your cake about 1–2 hours before carving it.

To create this cake...

- Base cake, made of four or five 20cm (8in) round cakes stacked together (should be 20cm/8in high)
- Middle tier cake, 15cm (6in) round cake, 10cm (4in) high
- Top tier cake, 10cm (4in) round cake, 7.5cm (3in) high
- 1.2kg (2lb 10½oz) untinted buttercream to fill and cover the cakes
- 300g (10½oz) light green buttercream (Sugarflair Gooseberry)
- 100g (3½oz) black buttercream (Sugarflair Black)
- 100–200g (3½–7oz) light green buttercream (Sugarflair Gooseberry)
- 100–200g (3½–7oz) dark green buttercream (Sugarflair Spruce Green)
- 200–300g (7–10½oz) yellow buttercream (Sugarflair Melon plus Autumn Leaf)
- 100–200g (3½–7oz) yellow-orange buttercream (Sugarflair Melon plus Tangerine)
- 100–200g (3½–7oz) orange buttercream (Sugarflair Tangerine)
- 100–200g (3½–7oz) blue buttercream (Sugarflair Baby Blue)
- 100–200g (3½–7oz) deep purple buttercream (Sugarflair Deep Purple plus Grape Violet)
- 100–200g (3½–7oz) light violet buttercream (Sugarflair Grape Violet)
- 100–150g (3½–5½oz) brown buttercream (Sugarflair Gooseberry plus Dark Brown)
- Paper or thin cardboard
- Scissors
- Long sharp pastry (serrated) knife
- 2 cake cards, at least 13 x 13cm (5 x 5in)
- 25cm (10in) cake drum
- 15cm (6in) round cake drum
- Palette knife
- Cake scraper
- Piping bags
- 4 dowel rods, plastic or wooden
- Ruler
- Wire cutters or big scissors

CREATING THE BASE CAKE

1. Stack and fill your cake beforehand and freeze it for about 1–2 hours. Trim a cake card to make a 13cm (5in) circle and place it as a guide centrally on top of your cake. Hold your knife at an angle and start cutting the corners of the cake at about 1cm (½in) all the way around.

2. Place a cake board on top of the cake and slide your hand under the bottom of the cake and quickly but carefully flip the cake over.

3. Trim another cake card to make a 10cm (4in) circle, place on top of the cake and repeat the same process. Carve the cake carefully to make it round, and make sure that the middle of the cake has a 20cm (8in) diameter. Crumb coat and chill for about thirty minutes to an hour.

4. Apply a layer of light green buttercream, and use a palette knife to spread it evenly all over the cake (see Covering Cakes). Add texture by stroking upwards with your palette knife – all your final strokes should be made with an upward motion.

5. Insert a dowel to measure the height of the cake. Pull it out and cut it and a further two dowels to the same size. Insert these three dowels and leave a space for a central dowel in the middle of the cake.

TIP

As a general guide, the diameter of the top of the ball cake needs to be no more than 5cm (2in) smaller than the diameter of the middle tier, and the base diameter, 2.5cm (1in) smaller than the middle tier for good support. If you are worried that the ball cake bottom tier will be squashed, dowel it as shown or substitute it with a denser material such as rice crispie cake or a polysterene cake dummy.

THE MIDDLE AND TOP TIERS

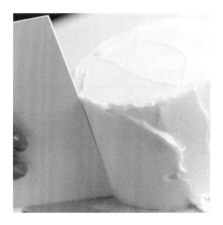

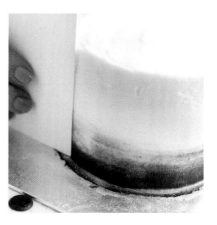

1. Remember to make a hole in the 15cm (6in) cake board for your central dowel. Place the middle tier cake on the board, cover with black buttercream and give it a smooth finish (see Covering Cakes). Cover your top tier cake with another layer of plain buttercream and even it out using your cake scraper.

2. Use a piping bag to apply a thin layer of black buttercream in a narrow strip around the bottom of the top tier cake.

3. Using your palette knife, spread the black buttercream slightly using an upward motion. Do not overdo it as it could make your cake look very messy.

4. Run your scraper around the top tier cake continuously in one direction to smooth it.

5. Stack the middle and top tiers together, then place them on top of the base cake and insert the central dowel all the way through the bottom to keep the cakes in place.

ADDING THE FLOWERS

1. Decide where you want to position your foliage and pipe it directly on to the cake (see Leaves).

2. Next, pipe the long and tall types of flowers. We have chosen snapdragon and brunnera, the instructions for which can be found in the Flowers section.

3. Next pipe the begonia, sunflower and clematis. You must pipe a blob of buttercream as a base for each of these blooms, in order to position them at the correct angle on the cake.

Opulent Cake

Elegant and luxurious, this three tiered design would make a perfect wedding cake, especially if the bride and groom want to avoid traditional royal icing or sugarpaste. The intricate patterning on the surface is made with an impression mat and highlighted in gold – what could be more appropriate for such a special occasion? This cake is completed with pure white Lilies, Gardenia and Magnolias.

CREATING THE DECORATIVE SURFACE

1. Fill and cover your cakes as normal (see Covering Cakes). You can either stack them together straight away or texture and airbrush them individually before stacking. When the cake surface is properly crusted (see tip), firmly press the impression mat against the surface of the cake. Repeat the process until the whole cake is textured. You can then stack them if you haven't done so.

2. To airbrush your cake with gold, never start spraying directly on to your cake as you may get a sudden burst of colour. Instead, start spraying onto a spare piece of paper first and then, whilst spraying, guide your spray onto your project. Don't spray too close to the cake's surface as your colour will be too dark – but spray too far away and it will be too light. Try your technique on paper first.

TIP
You must leave your cake to crust properly before using the impression mat otherwise it will stick. This can take anything between 15 and 30 minutes, sometimes longer, depending on temperature and humidity. Dusting your impression mat with cornflour (cornstarch) or icing sugar (confectioners' sugar) will help to prevent it sticking.

ADDING THE LEAVES AND FLOWERS

1. Pipe the stems and dark green leaves directly onto the sides of the cake (see Leaves).

2. Next, pipe lily of the valley and calla lilies directly onto the cake surface (see Flowers).

3. Pipe random blobs and position the gardenias and magnolias (see Flowers). It is helpful to freeze a small rose-like bud for the centre of the gardenia (see Freezing), position it on to the cake, then pipe petals around it.

4. To give height to the flowers, instead of piping a big blob of buttercream for the top of the cake, cut a small piece of sponge cake then cover it with buttercream.

5. Continue to pipe the rest of the flowers until all the gaps are filled. Lastly, pipe more leaves randomly.

To create this cake...

- Bottom tier cake, 20cm (8in) square cake, 18cm (7in) high
- Middle tier cake, 15cm (6in) square cake, 12.5cm (5in) high
- Top tier cake, 10cm (4in) square cake, 10cm (4in) high
- 1.6–2kg (3lb 8oz–4lb 8oz) buttercream to fill and cover the cake
- 1.2–1.5kg (2lb 10½oz–3lb 5oz) white buttercream (Sugarflair Super White)
- 500–800g (1lb 2oz–1lb 12oz) light green buttercream (Sugarflair Gooseberry)
- 500–800g (1lb 2oz–1lb 12oz) dark green buttercream (Sugarflair Spruce Green)
- 200–400g (7–14oz) yellow buttercream (Sugarflair Melon plus Autumn Leaf)
- 100–150g (3½–5½oz) brown buttercream (Sugarflair Gooseberry plus Dark Brown)
- Cake dowels, twelve 10cm (4in) for the cake tiers and one 38cm (15in) central dowel
- Cake drum, 25cm (10in) square
- Cake boards, 20cm (8in), 15cm (6in) and 10cm (4in) square
- Plastic impression mat
- Cornflour (cornstarch) or icing sugar (confectioners' sugar) for dusting
- Airbrush machine
- Edible gold airbrush liquid or gold lustre spray
- Piping bags
- Scissors
- Wilton Petal Nozzle 104
- Wilton Leaf Nozzle 352
- Wilton 81 Nozzle
- Wilton Leaf Nozzle 126

Ombre Cake

The astonishingly rich variety of flowers that tumble down the sides of this cake are certain to impress. Reds, purples, pinks and violets combine to dizzying effect. The clean lines of the ultra smooth background are the perfect backdrop to all that abundance of flora!

CREATING A SMOOTH SURFACE

1. After crumb coating your cake, chill it for 10 to 15 minutes or until the first coating of buttercream is firm. Then apply another layer all over the surface of the cake. Spread the buttercream evenly and take off any excess.

2. Run the scraper around the cake to get rid of any excess and leave an even thickness of buttercream all over your cake.

TIP
When covering the cake, make sure to get rid of all the excess buttercream so that you will be able to get sharp edges.

3. Leave to crusts then smooth with a non-woven cloth (interfacing) as follows: put the cloth on the surface of the cake and rub using your fingers and palm until it is nearly smooth. To make it perfectly smooth, use your cake scraper and stroke it up and down, finishing with upward strokes so all the excess will go to the edge of the cake.

4. Remove all the excess buttercream by cutting through it using a palette knife, a small paring knife or your scraper. Then repeat the smoothing process until the cake surface is perfect.

ADDING THE FLOWERS AND FOLIAGE

1. Make some amaranthus, bouvardia, ranunculus, roses and ornamental kale (see Flowers) on a flower nail and put them in the freezer (see Freezing). Then pipe all the lavenders, freesias, stems and buds.

2. Pipe blobs to mark the placement of flowers and to determine their angle. Add the pre-frozen flowers. To reposition a frozen flower without melting it, use two cocktails sticks (toothpicks) poked into the sides of the flower to move it about.

3. Add the flowers in this order: freesias, carnation leaves, carnations, violet leaves, poppies, violets, then pipe leaves randomly to complete the design.

To create this cake...

- Bottom tier cake, 20cm (8in) round cake, 6in high
- Middle tier cake, 15cm (6in) round cake, 20cm (8in) high
- Top tier cake, 10cm (4in) round cake, 10cm (4in) high
- 1.6–2kg (3lb 8oz–4lb 8oz) buttercream to fill and cover the cake
- 1.5–1.7kg (3lb 5oz–3lb 12oz) cream buttercream (Sugarflair Cream)
- 500–800g (1lb 2oz–1lb 12oz) light violet buttercream (Sugarflair Grape Violet)
- 500–800g (1lb 2oz–1lb 12oz) dark violet buttercream (Sugarflair Grape Violet)
- 500–800g (1lb 2oz–1lb 12oz) pink buttercream (Sugarflair Claret)
- 500–800g (1lb 2oz–1lb 12oz) light pink buttercream (Sugarflair Pastel Baby Pink)
- 500–800g (1lb 2oz–1lb 12oz) dark green buttercream (Sugarflair Spruce Green)
- 500–800g (1lb 2oz–1lb 12oz) light green buttercream (Sugarflair Gooseberry)
- 100–150g (3½–5½oz) black buttercream (Sugarflair Black)
- Cake dowels, four 15cm (6in) for bottom tier, four 10cm (4in) for middle tier, four 7.5cm (3in) and one 41cm (16in) central dowel
- Cake drum, 25cm (10in) square
- Cake boards, two 15cm (6in) and one 10cm (4in) round
- Cake scraper
- Non-woven cloth (interfacing)
- Piping bags
- Scissors
- Wilton Petal Nozzle 103
- Wilton Petal Nozzle 104
- Wilton Leaf Nozzle 352
- Wilton Leaf Nozzle 126
- PME Nozzle 57R
- PME Nozzle 32R
- PME Nozzle 42

Rustic Cake

Here's something completely different. By blending natural shades with a palette knife, we have created a life-like silver birch stump on which a selection of succulents and bright yellow flowers look perfectly at home. The blending effect is not hard to achieve, as long as you don't over-do it. Less is more for this unusual and intriguing design.

CREATING THE RUSTIC BACKGROUND

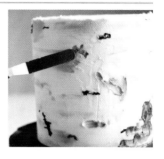

1. Crumb coat your cakes (see Covering Cakes). Use your palette knife to apply enough light grey buttercream to cover the cakes, then use the cake scraper to evenly distribute it all over.

2. Apply small amounts of darker grey buttercream randomly and smudge the colour using your palette knife.

3. Run your scraper around the cake in one direction, either clockwise or counter-clockwise. You can scrape it bit by bit using short strokes (see tip).

4. Repeat the same process with black and caramel buttercream. Do not overdo it, but aim for a realistic colouring.

5. Using black buttercream, add few random horizontal lines all around your cake, then scrape these too.

6. Apply dark yellow buttercream on top of the cake in a circular motion, then use a palette knife to spread it. Use a circular motion to give the impression of concentric tree stump rings.

7. Use a cocktail stick (toothpick) and make random dents to give a peeled bark effect.

TIP
When blending the colours, it is not necessary to run the scraper all the way round the cake in one go. You may make shorter strokes, as long as they are horizontal and in one direction only.

ADDING THE FOLIAGE AND FLOWERS

1. Stack the cakes, then start the decorative elements by piping the ferns.

2. Make and freeze the echeveria (see Freezing) then position them on the cake. If you need to manipulate them into position push two cocktail sticks (toothpicks) into the sides, rather than using your warm fingers. Make sure to pipe blobs of buttercream underneath them to give depth.

3. Pipe the other succulents directly onto the side of the cake, then the craspedia, buttercups, and random leaves (see Leaves) using dark green buttercream.

To create this cake...

- Bottom tier cake, 20cm (8in) round cake, 20cm (8in) high
- Top tier cake, 15cm (6in) round cake, 10cm (4in) high
- 600–800g (1lb 5oz–1lb 12oz) untinted buttercream to fill the cake
- 800g–1kg (1lb 12oz–2lb 4oz) light grey buttercream (Sugarflair Pastel Shadow Grey)
- 200–300g (7–10½oz) grey buttercream (Sugarflair Pastel Shadow Grey)
- 500–800g (1lb 2oz–1lb 12oz) yellow buttercream (Sugarflair Melon)
- 800g–1kg (1lb 12oz–2lb 4oz) dark yellow buttercream (Sugarflair Melon plus Autumn Leaf)
- 100–200g (3½–7oz) pink buttercream (Sugarflair Claret)
- 200–300g (7–10½oz) caramel buttercream (Sugarflair Caramel)
- 500–800g (1lb 2oz–1lb 12oz) dark green buttercream (Sugarflair Spruce Green)
- 500–800g (1lb 2oz–1lb 12oz) light green buttercream (Sugarflair Gooseberry)
- 100–150g (3½–5½oz) black buttercream (Sugarflair Black)
- Cake dowels, eight 10cm (4in) for the bottom tier and one 30cm (12in) central dowel
- Cake drum, 25cm (10in) round
- Cake boards, 20cm (8in) and 15cm (6in) round
- Cake scraper
- Piping bags
- Scissors
- Wilton Petal Nozzle 103
- Wilton Petal Nozzle 104
- Wilton Leaf Nozzle 352
- Wilton Leaf Nozzle 126
- PME Nozzle 57R
- PME Nozzle 32R
- PME Nozzle 42

Vintage Cake

The lovely retro quality of this cake is created with a delightfully dotty background and clusters of cheerfully bright flowers that would not look out of place on a piece of vintage china. Using a paper pattern makes the dotted design easy to achieve. You could try this design in pastel shades for a softer, but still charmingly old-fashioned look.

CREATING THE DOTTED PATTERN

1. Cover the top and bottom tiers with light blue buttercream and the middle tier with mid blue (see Covering Cakes). Decide how many dots you want, and draft the pattern on paper first before marking it out on the cake (see tip).

2. Use light blue buttercream in a piping bag with a small hole at the tip to pipe the dots.

TIP
To mark a pattern, take a piece of paper the exact size of the side of the cake and draft your design before transferring it to your cake. Do this by pricking through the paper pattern with a round-headed pin to make guide marks in the buttercream on the cake. You can pre-prick the holes in the paper first, then just slide the pin through, making the job easier. If your cake is round, use a continuous strip of greaseproof (wax) paper to measure the circumference of the cake. Then draft your design on that paper before you mark your cake.

ADDING THE FLOWERS AND FOLIAGE

1. Look at your cake as one big canvas. Make marks with buttercream or a cocktail stick (toothpick), to show where you will position your flowers. Try to balance the spaces in between them.

2. Pipe the marigold, then the buddleia (see Flowers).

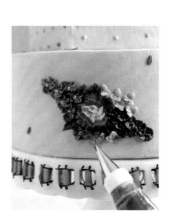

3. Pipe the small brunnera, then the hypericum berries and then the leaves.

4. Repeat the same process and pipe the flowers in the same order all over the top tier and around the bottom tier.

To create this cake...

- Bottom tier cake, 20cm (8in) round cake, 12.5cm (5in) high
- Middle tier cake, 15 x 15cm (6 x 6in) square cake, 12.5cm (5in) high
- Top tier cake, 10cm (4in) round cake, 10cm (4in) high
- 800g–1kg (1lb 12oz–2lb 4oz) untinted buttercream to fill and crumb coat the cake
- 800g–1kg (1lb 12oz–2lb 4oz) light blue buttercream (Sugarflair Baby Blue plus a hint of Navy Blue)
- 300–500g (10½oz–1lb 2oz) mid blue buttercream (Sugarflair Baby Blue plus hint of Navy Blue)
- 400–600g (14oz–1lb 5oz) dark blue buttercream (Sugarflair Baby Blue plus Navy Blue)
- 300–500g (10½oz–1lb 2oz) blue buttercream (Sugarflair Deep Purple)
- 300–500g (10½oz–1lb 2oz) light green buttercream (Sugarflair Gooseberry)
- 300–500g(10½oz–1lb 2oz) dark green buttercream (Sugarflair Spruce Green)
- 250–350g (9–12oz) light orange buttercream (Sugarflair Orange plus Melon)
- 250–350g (9–12oz) dark orange buttercream (Sugarflair Orange plus Red)
- Cake dowels, four 10cm (4in) for the bottom tier, four 12.5cm (5in) for the middle tier and one 30cm (12in) central dowel
- Cake drum, 20cm (8in) round
- Cake boards, 15cm (6in) round and 15cm (6in) square
- Piping bags
- Scissors
- Ruler
- Paper
- Pen
- Round-headed pin
- Cocktail stick (toothpick)
- Wilton Petal Nozzle 103
- Wilton Leaf Nozzle 352
- PME Nozzle 57R
- PME Nozzle 58R

SUPPLIERS

UK SUPPLIERS

Squires Kitchen Sugarcraft Ltd
The Grange, Hones Yard, Farnham, Surrey GU9 8BB
+44 (0)1252 260260
www.squires-shop.com
Big selection of cake decorating supplies and food colours

Edible Creators Ltd
191 Station Road, Rainham, Kent ME8 7SQ
+44 (0)1634 235407 / 07581 395801
www.ediblecreatorsltd.com
Supplier of impression mats and texture sheets

Wilton UK
Merlin Park, Wood Lane, Erdington, Birmingham B24 9QL
+44 (0)121 386 3200
www.wilton.co.uk
Big selection of nozzles and cake decorating materials

Doric FPD (Food Packaging and Decorations)
Farrington Road, Rossendale Road Industrial Estate, Burnley,
Lancashire BB11 5SW
+44 (0)1282 423142
www.doriccakecrafts.co.uk
Supplier of food packaging and cake decorating materials

Cake Stuff Ltd
Milton Industrial Estate, Lesmahagow, Scotland ML11 0JN
+44 (0)1555 890111
www.cake-stuff.com
Supplier of cake decorating materials

Sugar and Crumbs Ltd
3 Grove Road, Wrexham LL11 1DY
+44 (0)161 449 7976
www.sugarandcrumbs.co.uk
Supplier of natural flavoured icing sugar, cocoa powder and
sugarpaste

DinkyDoodle Designs
2b Triumph Road, Nottingham NG7 2GA
+44 (0)115 969 9803
www.dinkydoodledesigns.co.uk
Supplier of airbrush machines and colours

Knightsbridge PME Ltd
Riverwalk Business Park, Riverwalk Rd, Enfield EN3 7QN
+44 (0)20 3234 0049
www.knightsbridgepme.co.uk

US SUPPLIERS

The Cake World
184 Broadway #15 (Route 1N) - Saugus, MA 01906 – 781-558-5508
+1 781-558-5508
www.thecakeworld.net
Supplier of cake decorating materials

ABC Cake Decorating Supplies/Cake Art
2853 E Indian School Rd, Phoenix, AZ 85016
+1 602-224-9796
www.cakearts.com
Supplier of cake decorating materials and edible printing

The Wilton Store
7511 Lemont Road, Darien IL 60561
+1 630-985-6000
www.wilton.com
Big selection of nozzles and cake decorating supplies

ACKNOWLEDGMENTS

We would like to thank our publisher, F&W Media, for giving us the chance to write our second book. To the wonderful team there: Ame Verso, Honor Head, Charlotte Andrew, Emma Gardner, Jo Lystor and Sam Vallance. To our ever patient project editor, Jane Trollope, thank you for replying to all our queries even on a Sunday. To our photographer, Jack Kirby, thank you for making our photoshoot sessions such a breeze.

We will be forever grateful to Cake International organizers: Clare Fisher, Ben Fidler, David Bennet, Melanie Underwood, Troy Bennet, Simon Burns and everyone else, as they were the first who invested trust in us and allowed us to showcase our talents to the world. We would also like to thank all the hosts of our international classes for helping us spread BUTTERCREAM LOVE in their respective countries.

To our increasing number of friends and followers around the world, we thank you all from the bottom of our hearts for your continuous support and for being such a huge part of our cake journey. You brought us to where we are now.

To our families back in the Philippines, thank you for being the best fan group ever. We hope that we always make you proud and we dedicate this book to all of you.

ABOUT THE AUTHORS

Valeri Valeriano and Christina Ong left the Philippines in 2008 to work in the UK in the medical field. After the 'sweet accident' of learning how to make cupcake bouquets in 2011, they launched their business Queen of Hearts Couture Cakes and have since won several top awards in various prestigious cake competitions.

Now renowned globally for their edible works of art, using nothing else but buttercream as their decorating medium, Valeri and Christina have been featured in numerous well-known magazines and on local and international news. They have appeared on television, and showcased their masterpieces and demonstrated their craft in major cake shows in the UK and abroad. They hold masterclasses in the UK, Europe, Asia and the US and have also held a couple of masterclasses at the famous Victoria & Albert Museum, London.

Valeri and Christina take immense pride in their mastery of buttercream art and this makes Queen of Hearts Couture Cakes exclusive. They have modernized what is commonly known as the age-old art of buttercream, and this is reflected in their creations. Their cake designs are elegant, original and eminently contemporary.

Find out more at
www·queenofheartscouturecakes·com and **www· facebook·com/QueenofHeartsCupcakesAndMore**

INDEX

A DAVID & CHARLES BOOK
© F&W Media International, Ltd 2015

David & Charles is an imprint of F&W Media International, Ltd
Brunel House, Forde Close, Newton Abbot, TQ12 4PU, UK

F&W Media International, Ltd is a subsidiary of F+W Media, Inc
10151 Carver Road, Suite #200, Blue Ash, OH 45242, USA

A catalogue record for this book is available from the
British Library.

ISBN-13: 978-1-4463-0574-4 paperback
ISBN-10: 1-4463-0574-0 paperback

ISBN-13: 978-1-4463-7086-5 PDF
ISBN-10: 1-4463-7086-0 PDF

ISBN-13: 978-1-4463-7085-8 EPUB
ISBN-10: 1-4463-7085-2 EPUB

Printed in USA by RR Donnelley for:
F&W Media International, Ltd
Brunel House, Forde Close, Newton Abbot, TQ12 4PU, UK

10 9 8 7 6 5 4 3

Content Director: Ame Verso
Editors: Charlotte Andrew and Emma Gardner
Project Editor: Jane Trollope
Art Editor: Jodie Lystor
Photographer: Jack Kirby
Production Manager: Beverley Richardson

F+W Media publishes high quality books on a wide
range of subjects.
For more great book ideas visit: www.stitchcraftcreate.co.uk

Layout of the digital edition of this book may vary depending on
reader hardware and display settings.